PAUL
A Man Who Changed the World

PAUL

A
Man
Who
Changed
the
World

by Henrietta Buckmaster

McGraw-Hill Book Company: New York, Toronto, London

For Waldemar

CONTENTS

A FEW WORDS TO THE READER

No individual in history, except Jesus and possibly Shakespeare, seems to have prompted so many books, commentaries, essays and exegeses as the man we know as Paul the apostle to the Gentiles. Today eighty-three books in print about him testify to his significance and fascination.

The reasons perhaps are obvious. Paul was the architect of Christianity. Almost every human being in the western world has been influenced by his understanding of the Christ. Few other men have set up such conflicts of love and despair. "Whether we are conscious of it or not, he has left a mark—his own individual mark—upon our life; our recurrent attempts to understand him are a part of our continuing effort to understand ourselves," John Knox of Union Theological Seminary wrote in *Life* not long ago.

Our sources are both rich and elusive. Our primary means for knowing him are the nine epistles which are, in general, accepted as Pauline: *Romans, I* and *II Corinthians, Galatians, Philippians, Colossians, I* and *II Thessalonians, Philemon,* although some of these have half-hearted supporters who feel that fragments only belong to Paul. (*I Thessalonians* is, as far as we know, the earliest surviving piece of Christian literature.) Our secondary source is *The Acts of the Apostles* written, it is usually agreed, by a Greek Christian named Luke after Paul's death.

From this modest but remarkable basis the enormous body of literature on Paul has been brought into existence. When embarking on any study of Paul it is essential to keep in mind that what has been written relies heavily on speculation, however well informed and brilliant. As one who has read scores of books on the man and his thought, I suspect that all books on

Paul are to a degree highly subjective—beginning with *The Acts of the Apostles* and including, for the sake of honesty, this one.

All efforts to understand a man's place in history necessarily go through this process. He must be seen through a thousand eyes, through pragmatic, spiritual, parochial, universal points of view; and in time his reality may suffer such a sea change that he becomes a shifting symbol. I do not feel there is anything wrong about this. It seems to be inevitable that what an individual has brought to life must, in the end, be judged by intrinsic values and these values then shaped to deepening needs and insights. Yet somewhere there is also an unchanging core of truth.

Reading in the epistles Paul's account of an event and comparing it with the account given in *Acts* makes one feel sometimes that he is reading about two different men and events. (This problem is discussed vividly and cogently in *The Interpreters' Bible*, Volume 9, and in *Chapters in the Life of Paul* by John Knox.) Because of this, scholars once questioned the reliability of *Acts*; textual differences and translations compounded a mischief, but modern historiography is bringing new tools to the resolution of such difficulties. Archaeology, sociology with its historic perceptions, anthropology, psychology are striking much closer to that core of truth than did the earlier theological attitudes which were frequently concerned to support a point of view or anxious to turn Paul into a nineteenth century Lutheran or Presbyterian.

Of course no scholar is immune to the urge to create attractive hypotheses to explain gaps in our knowledge—hypotheses which may become confused with pragmatic evidence. But understanding comes along many paths. I am not a theologian, nor even a scholar in a formal sense of the word. But I am trained, as is every serious writer, to discipline ideas and measure facts with a cool and careful eye. I am also profoundly aware that probabilities and an informed and guarded imagination must supplement those tools of the historiographer if some semblance of a whole is to be invoked. Many "biographies" of Paul have taken little account of the world in which he lived. Yet he, in common with every human being, was deeply affected by the time in which he lived, by the tensions and pressures of a world shaken by change, and by the divine inspirations which had been released into this world.

If we can understand and measure these pressures, negative and positive, comprehend to some degree the explosive nature of Christianity, love and evaluate this man—all within the context of his world and in relation to the years of his ministry—we will begin to understand in many subtle and significant ways the dimensions of his spiritual genius as it relates to us in this age.

For purposes of readability, I have avoided the use of "probably" and "it is thought" and all such safeguards of scholarship. However I am well aware that categoric statements must be taken with reservations. Our only first-hand facts about Paul are his own statements in the epistles which, in turn, are partisan —he is defending a course of action with all his might.

When I say "Paul came to Ephesus with the fall rains," this should be read as a probability, based on one's knowledge of seasonal travel in the Mediterranean world in Roman times. When Luke joins a scene, I am sharing in the assumption (by no means supported by all scholars) that the "we" sections of *Acts*, starting at 16:10, indicate personal participation by Luke. When I confidently attribute verses from *II Timothy* to Paul, I am perfectly aware that the Pastoral Epistles—*I* and *II Timothy* and *Titus*—are now believed (from good internal evidence) to belong to a much later period; but original Pauline fragments, which carry the strong tone of Paul's voice, may have been included in *II Timothy*.

To anyone wishing to enlarge his knowledge of Paul I recommend first of all the General Articles and exegeses found in

The Interpreters' Bible, which includes not only two translations but the best of modern theological scholarship. These volumes are invaluable. For an historical background which illuminates the Pauline age, the books of Josephus: *The Wars of the Jews* and *Antiquities*—now over eighteen hundred years old—are unfailingly stimulating. *Primitive Christianity in Its Contemporary Setting* by Rudolph Bultmann, *Earliest Christianity* by Johannes Weiss, *Paul* by Adolph Deissmann, *Light from the Ancient Past* by Jack Finegan, *Caesar and Christ* by Will Durant, are rich in background and lore. The readability and rigorous scholarship of Morton Scott Enslin's *Christian Beginnings* illumines modern theological thinking.

The titles in the bibliography are self-explanatory: *On Roman Roads with St. Paul, Beyond Damascus*, and the others listed are extremely helpful in providing details of the past. H. V. Morton's *In the Steps of Paul* and Freya Stark's beautiful books of travel in the Aegean world, *Ionia* and *The Lycian Shore*, are filled with insights and with senses and sensibilities which carry one back two thousand years. Sir William Ramsay's two great books on his archaeological work in Turkey and his study of documents are mountain peaks in our understanding of Paul.

My bibliography is merely a starter, the books listed having on the whole the virtue of modesty.

I have not indicated the translations of the epistles or *Acts* which I have used because there seemed no appropriate way to do so without burdening the reader. I have browsed, let us say, from the King James through the Revised to the New English to Sir William Ramsay's own translations, and have made my selections where a captured subtlety of meaning or clarity of expression seemed most apt.

In the study of Paul there is, and always has been, infinite latitude. This latitude should be used to the full in order to sense the full scope of this incomparable man.

H.B.

PRINCIPAL SOURCES

Booth, Henry Kendall, *The World of Jesus* (Scribner's, 1933)

Bowra, Cecil Maurice, *The Greek Experience* (Mentor, 1960)

Bultmann, Rudolph, *Primitive Christianity in Its Contemporary Setting* (Meridian, 1956)

Buttrick, George A., ed. *Interpreters' Bible* (Abingdon, 1951-57)

Deissmann, Adolph, *Paul: A Study in Social and Religious History* (Harper, 1957)

Durant, Will, *Story of Civilization, Vol. 3, Caesar and Christ* (Simon and Schuster, 1944)

Enslin, Morton Scott, *Christian Beginnings* (Harper, 1956)

Enslin, Morton Scott, *The Ethics of Paul* (Abingdon, 1962)

Finegan, Jack, *Light from the Ancient Past* (Princeton, 1959)

Goodspeed, Edgar J., *Paul, a Biography* (Holt, Rinehart & Winston, 1948)

Kent, Charles Foster, *Biblical Geography and History* (Scribner's, 1920)

Klausner, Joseph, *From Jesus to Paul* (Macmillan, 1943)

Knox, John, *Chapters in a Life of Paul* (Abingdon, 1950)

Metzger, Henri, *St. Paul's Journeys in the Greek Orient* (Philosophical Library, 1956)

Morton, H. V., *In the Steps of Paul* (Dodd, 1936)

Nock, Arthur Darby, *St. Paul* (Harper, 1948)

Pope, Robert Martin, *On Roman Roads with St. Paul* (Epworth, 1939)

Ramsay, William M., *The Cities of St. Paul*, with *St. Paul, the Traveler and the Roman Citizen* (Baker Book House, 1960)

Spencer, Floyd Albert, *Beyond Damascus* (Harper, 1934)

Weiss, Johannes, *Earliest Christianity* (Harper, 1959)

Whiston, William, tr., *Life and Work of Josephus* (Winston, 1936)

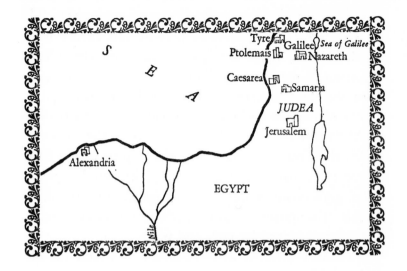

1

JERUSALEM
The World Waits

The sun, rising, shone on the black mountains of Greece, and on all the white temples on hills and seawashed thrusts of land.

The sun, setting, darkened the long golden shore of Asia Minor, where ancient gods, indistinguishable from the earth, had corroded time. It cast the shadow of the Roman garrison across the Temple in Jerusalem.

The Aegean flowed into the Mediterranean. The Mediterranean washed the shores of Palestine and Italy. This was a world of light, a world of the sea, of innumerable stars, where the mysteries of present and future were sought. Over it all lay the light of Hellenism, the culture and spirit of the Greeks, still luminous enough to obscure the ravages of poverty and the world's despair.

The end of the antique world had come with the rise of Alexander the Great. He had destroyed the old social order, the Greek city-states and the empires of the East. There each man and each god had known his place; tribal gods could be outwitted or fought to a standstill or left triumphant by other gods in the eternal battle for survival waged by gods and men.

Alexander brought a universalism in which the old gods could survive only if their individual functions were surrendered to a cosmic power variously called Zeus, Athena, Apollo, Serapis. This universalism acknowledged the old primordial needs, but within a theocracy which melded, blent, transmuted in a vivid eclecticism.

The power of the old gods was reinvested in god-sized men like Hercules or Aesculapius, in hero-deities like Sandon, in savior-godlings like Attis, Adonis, Tammuz. A belief in tribe or nation as the apotheosis of salvation had been broken so completely that salvation had become an individual matter. If the features of the Greek pantheon were coarsened by the infusion of many deities so, by the same token, the terrible Molochs and Baals and Marduks were subtilized by the new concepts.

Hellenism had determined the climate of civilized art, invention, and thinking. Powerful and diffusive by the second century B.C., it had invested the proud city of Jerusalem during the reign of the Syrian Antiochus Epiphanes, the Seleucid kinglet, seventh successor to one of Alexander's generals. Were it not for the Temple, Jerusalem might seem a Greek city. For this reason the Maccabees aroused the people to wrest Judea from the Syrian Greeks and to purify Judaism. Members of the family of the Maccabees assumed the High Priesthood, displacing Sadducees under whose authority Judaism had been made acceptable to the Hellenic world.

By the time of Julius Caesar the intense glory of Hellenism was fading though it still offered all that men knew of that objective supposition of which Sophocles spoke: "There are many strange wonders, but nothing more wonderful than man." All through the East the march of Rome was sounding. Rome, smashing the remnants of Alexander's empire, was approaching a mastery of the world. In 63 B.C. Judea fell to Rome. Pompey stood in the Holy of Holies and was astonished to find it empty.

Augustus Caesar proclaimed Roman peace for the world. Everywhere, from the ancient East to barbaric Britain, this peace quieted the nerves but did not answer the questions of life and death. Most men lived between fear of hunger and terror of death. But man, giving all his heart to placating the unappeasable, is a lonely figure. The self-sufficiency of the Stoics, the impassivity of the Epicureans, the asceticism of the Cynics, the causelessness of the Skeptics did not assuage that loneliness nor soften the harsh fact that half the men and women in the world were enslaved.

Only the Jews had continued to maintain their monotheistic wonder, their profound, unanthropomorphic concept of cause and effect, and this drew lonely seekers to the synagogues founded in many parts of the Eastern world by Jews dispersed by their conquerors.

"Who hath directed the Spirit of the Lord or being his counsellor hath taught him? . . . They that wait upon the Lord shall renew their strength; they shall mount up with wings as eagles; they shall run and not be weary, they shall run and not faint . . . God setteth the solitary in families."

The Jews did not eat with the Gentiles for fear of breaking a detail of the Law, but they compassed land and sea to save a soul. The Hellenists ate with the whole world and did not care what became of a man's soul.

Between the two spiritual peaks of Israel and Greece lay the empty void where superstition, necromancy, phallic worship, and all the stumbling fears of life and death fought for admission.

The Romans, masters of all that the eyes could see, measured, feared, and used them all.

Into this triple-pillared world Paul was born.

Paul was probably born sometime between 3 and 15 A.D. He himself said he came from Tarsus, "no mean city," was a freeborn Roman citizen, had been a student of the Rabbi Gamaliel, was a Pharisee of the Pharisees, and had harried the Christians to death in Jerusalem.

Some believe that Paul destroyed the Christianity of Jesus. Others believe that if it had not been for Paul, Christianity would have disappeared. Take whichever point of view you like, Paul was a man who changed the world.

Tarsus, with the Mediterranean at its feet, was a great port. Set in the flowering Cilician plain, with the river Cydnus flowing through the city, the snowy Taurus mountains at its back, its streets and buildings, its university and temple unrivaled in the East, Tarsus was a lodestar for merchants, philosophers, and the footloose rich who traveled tirelessly in pursuit of the sights.

Flax was grown in the fields. In the bitter mountain cold, rough long hair grew on the Cilician goats. Both flax and goat hair made the linen, tent- and sailcloth on which Tarsus built its fortune—perhaps even the fortune of Paul's family, for many scholars believe that his father was a rich man.

Pious Jews, rich or poor, were enjoined to teach their sons a trade to protect them from charity. Paul had been taught the trade of weaving, tent- and sailmaking —reasonable for the son of a textile maker.

The roots of the city were very gnarled and tangled. In the days before memory it had been a city of the Hittites. A pinion from the wings of Pegasus, falling to earth had brought its name—*tarsos*.

Now its language was Greek, but strange dialects from a forgotten time still floated like pollen in the city. Its appearance and administration were white, gleaming, and Roman. Its intellectual respectability rested on its love of the Greek philosophies. Its religious orthodoxy was confirmed by the temples to the correct pantheon and by the altars to the Emperor. (Roman Emperors had assumed the position of godhead so that Emperor-worship could act as a synthesis.)

The average Tarsian however put his greatest trust in the occult forces that lay in those ancient tangled roots of his memory.

He worshipped Hercules and Perseus, god-heroes who shifted like mist and became other ancient gods, and Sandon who had immolated himself by fire in a gesture of redemption. He worshipped the spirits of rivers, springs, and hills. He worshipped the Earth Mother, Cybele, who was queen of all. Cybele comforted women, reassured men. Her rites were phallic and orgiastic. Her priestesses were the Amazons, dressed in skins. Her processions through the streets of Tarsus were made to the shriek of pipes, the thunder of cymbals, the leaping of priests who emasculated themselves in public in imitation of Attis, her lover and husband.

In every fashionable garden (here and in Italy) was also an image of Priapus, that lewd and convivial little god of procreation, with his enormous genitals painted red. Tokens of Priapus were worn by the children to ward off bad luck, and Priapic symbols hung over the doors of houses and were engraved on tombstones.

In Tarsus was also the rich manipulation of miracle-workers, astrologers, interpreters of dreams, astral philosophers, Jewish occultists who had come under the influence of Persian mysticism.

Only the orthodox Jew put his life, his fortune, and his hope of salvation into a profound spiritual monotheism.

But though the Jew might go from home to synagogue to school with eyes averted, the din of procession in honor of the amative deities, the cries, the groans, the pungencies of seminal cults, the constant friction of the air, the relentless proselytising of both holy men and charlatans confirmed the Jew's long and painful necessity to "come out from among them and be separate."

This Tarsus was the city of Paul.

Paul called himself a Pharisee of the Pharisees. Phariseeism cooled and ordered the spirit. The Pharisees laid great stress on the ritual and forms of pious law. In defense of Judaism they evolved a great body of precepts which went beyond the law of Moses. If law—religious, civil, criminal—was God's communication to the sons of Israel, law must be observed in every jot and tittle in order to prepare for the day when His might and majesty filled the world.

The laws of purity were so exact and minute that any contact with the Gentiles—that is, the uncircumcised—became completely untenable. The Jew stood, against his will, in the cloaca of the world; he was surrounded on all sides by the polytheism and phallic cults of the pagans who made immorality a virtue, and for this reason he saw his law, his nation, his hope of salvation preserved only by the most rigorous adherence to the law. Circumcision was the mark of his covenant with God. It was the token of purity. To the Greek world, however, circumcision was a mutilation of the body almost as distasteful as the emasculation of priests.

In the fear, disillusionment and decay, the golden splendor, the Greek languor, the political expediencies, the fixed requirements of Jewish law, the cold watchfulness of Rome, there was little place for the spirit. An echo of spirit was heard each morning when the priests in Jerusalem greeted the dawn with the invocation of Israel, *Hear, O Israel, the Lord our God, the Lord is One,* but was lost again when the gates swung open on the cold mechanism of temple worship. Spiritual power was nursed in the little synagogues scattered about the Mediterranean, or by lonely men waiting for the Messiah.

But this was a world of remorseless pressures, the climax of change reaching into the most obscure details of a man's life. Idealism was paid for at a very high price. All who carried the mark of circumcision waited for the consolation of Israel, the king of the line of David who would subdue all people under the sign of Emmanuel. All signs indicated that the day of the Messiah was near. But to the Jews who loved the hope and the promise there was no trace of the king foretold by prophecy in the voluptuous orientalism of the Herodians.

Jewish patriots, committed to the overthrow of Roman power in Judea, had taken the name of Zealots. Those

Zealots who hid in the hills and ambushed the Roman soldiers became known as Assassins. Bands of Daggermen roamed the cities punishing with death Romans and sycophants and two high priests.

The Romans hated Judea, with its strong invisible god and its intractable people, for the most sophisticated political opposition in the empire came from Judea. But the Romans had political cunning. They turned to the Sadducees and the Sadducean High Priests to carry out their orders.

The Romans knew that power challenged power and that a king of the Jews might come in the dark of the night, but they would be waiting.

Under Caesar Augustus there had been many Jewish uprisings. When Herod the Great died, and a revolt was raised against his successor, three thousand Jews were killed at the Passover festival. And when the Pentecost was celebrated, many more were put to death, the Temple cloisters burned to the ground by the Romans and the sanctuary treasures looted. Patriots turned into shifting, disappearing armies; Judas the Gaulonite, commanding such an army, seized Sepphoris the capital of Galilee.

The Romans brought up twenty thousand men from Syria to support the Herodian claim and put down the rebellion. Hundreds of towns in Galilee were burned to the ground. Thirty thousand Jews were sold into slavery, and two thousand were crucified in a monstrous collective death.

Then Augustus withdrew the kingdom from the Herodians and sent a procurator to rule under the Roman proconsul of Syria.

In the Temple, sacrifices were made to Jehovah in the name of the Emperor—an agreement of desperate expediency to prevent a more intolerable demand.

Disquiet was everywhere. There was much waiting. Certain fresh winds seemed to spring from nowhere. What they would bring in and what they would take away were still imperceptible in the heavy air.

At length Jesus came out of Nazareth. He was seen and heard for three seasons of plowing and harvest. Zealots had watched him and waited for a sign (Simon the Zealot was among his disciples). Rabbis had come to him, and common men and women. They asked if he were the Messiah.

He had not raised a sword. He had said, "My kingdom is not of this world," and yet he had claimed the Messiahship. This was sedition to the Zealots if not to the Romans, for it set the simple pragmatism of political action sadly awry. Yet when Pontius Pilate, the Roman procurator, asked him if he were King of the Jews he said that he was. He condemned himself by his own mouth. He had said, "Everyone that is of the truth heareth my voice," and Pilate asked the Greek question, "What is truth?"

Pilate, asking such a question, must have known how often truth was hanged. "This is the King of the Jews" nailed above Jesus' head on the cross was the sardonic Roman warning that men cannot have it both ways. If their king were killed there was no more king against Caesar.

The cross was a curse. To the Jew, a curse was not merely a mental condition; it was a generative poison that affected the atmosphere about it. An executed criminal who was hanged on a tree suffered a special curse and shockingly defiled the air and the ground on which his shadow fell. In Sepphoris, the two thousand crucified patriots had impregnated air and earth by the involuntary curse of their deaths, and all the land about them was abandoned. The Nazarenes who called this hanged and cursed man the Messiah of Jewish prophecy were guilty of an outrage too monstrous to reckon.

But he had not died. He grew larger and larger in the experiences of men and women. The Roman policy which had no use for subtlety or craftiness, but was very adroit, made no open comment. However, the Roman garrison in Antony's Tower looked down into the courtyard of the Temple and the High Priest was a Roman weathervane.

The High Priest served the Romans first, then the God of Israel. It was a political situation familiar in the world.

The Nazarene disciples who had been shaken by betrayal, doubt, and grief had been commanded to wait. They waited, like seeds in the ground. They had been children while he was here. While they waited they became men. Jesus had made an inviolate promise to come back. They stood with their faces to the sky for a long time.

As good Jews they had asked him, "Lord, wilt thou at this time restore the kingdom to Israel?" He had not promised. He had promised only patience and power and that "ye shall be witnesses unto me both in Jerusalem and in all Judea and in Samaria and unto the uttermost parts of the earth." They were simple men and they thought in simple terms and did not give up their expectation.

They lived in a community of fellowship. This fellowship and care for each other, the sharing of goods and breaking of bread was sublimely Jewish and then went on much further. It went into a world of simple love, inexpedient, tender, unified. It went out into a way of life—faith without works being dead.

They were good Jews. Those whom Jesus taught were seen daily in the Temple, walking and talking in the courts where the great rabbis gathered their students. Peter was not a great rabbi but he found the power of speech. When he healed a lame beggar well known to all at the Beautiful Gate of the Temple, it was clear that a sign of recurring truth, a new expectation, a messianic word was being offered to the sons of Israel. The cloud that had obscured the Christ had existed solely in the minds of men. Out of the wonder of the people who came running, Peter drew his first words, "Ye men of Israel, why marvel ye at this?"

Without works faith is dead. A lame man leaping to his feet was a lively synonym for the everpresence of the power of God shown by the "Prince of life" whom they had tried to kill.

It was an awkward speech Peter made, but with it he found his tongue. This young man, groping and grappling, waked authorities in the Temple. Since the crucifixion they had watched the Nazarenes, but with half an eye; now they swung around fullface. The lame man, leaping, liberated the apostles to see themselves as they were, formidable men, resounding with joy, speaking with confidence, acting like heirs of the future.

Jerusalem was a city filled with spies: spies Roman and Herodian, and spies of the High Priest. Now it seemed filled with Nazarenes spying out salvation.

The Temple guards put them in prison for the night. In the morning the leading members of the Sanhedrin, Sadducees, Pharisees, and the scribes who governed the people met with the High Priest. When the apostles stood before them they asked them sharply by what chicanery they had done this thing. Peter and John were prepared to answer the wind, the sun, the kings of the earth if they had asked. The man who had been lame stood beside them. It is high time, Peter said, "that you and all Israel knew that by the power of Jesus Christ of Nazareth—that cornerstone which you rejected—does this man stand before you whole."

The High Priest and the Sanhedrin had made inquiries again and again about these men. Nothing was hidden. They were what they said they were, peasants without education, yet they were prodigiously more. This fact was a miracle almost as great as the lame man walking. The lame man walked all around them. The authority of the High Priest, in his great turban, and the members of the Sanhedrin, in their prayer shawls was greatly diminished by this. They could not deny the remarkable healing, but they could not sanction it either. They spoke to these men severely, saying that they must not speak or act in the name of a man hanged from a cross.

But when Peter had found his tongue he had found it forever. Right or wrong, he said, we must tell what we know.

The High Priest let them go because everyone in the city had heard that the lame man was walking. Consider all this for a moment:

Jesus of Nazareth had been in Judea for three years doing remarkable things. This was in the prophetic line of inspiration, the glory of the Jews. But he had claimed the Messiahship and this had nailed him to a cross and a curse. Now these men who had been with him reproduced his actions and called upon his name for their authority. Were they also going to claim the Messiahship? The event by the Beautiful Gate was incomparable in its power to catch the heart, and the heart has never been a friend to authority.

After this, even more remarkable things took place. The High Priest knew that a tremulous status quo would not last five minutes if the Romans felt any alarm. When too many Jews began to talk about salvation and put their worldly possessions at the disciples' feet, laid their sick where the shadow of Peter would fall, came out from the Greek cities around Jerusalem bringing their sick, then a delicate political mechanism was in

danger and its custodians would be deficient in office
if they did not take alarm.

They acted with competence. Stephen, a Nazarene,
who some think came from Tarsus, had begun to debate
in the synagogues of Jerusalem. These synagogues were
the spiritual homes of the Hellenist Jews of the Diaspora
—those Jews who had been scattered among the Gentiles
after the Babylonian captivity. The Jew from Tarsus,
Cyrene, Libya, Egypt, Asia, worshipped in his own synagogue when he came to Jerusalem. Stephen said that
Jesus was the Messiah and Stephen also performed many
acts of spiritual power; he was clearly a man of grace and
persuasion.

In the free world of the synagogue he was master of
every debate. He spoke with reason and spiritual force,
and no son of Israel was born to resist this combination.
To silence him his message must be suborned. Men were
paid to say that he had blasphemed. Jerusalem was a city
too politically intelligent and thwarted not to be at the
mercy of every rumor, charge, and possibility. Stephen
was more dangerous than Peter, but at the same time
more vulnerable. None of the aura of discipleship lay
over him. He was merely a vivid, devoted, compelling,
heretical Jew who had the capacity to become a towering man.

Without warning he was seized and thrust before the
Sanhedrin.

His defense was as colorful as his debates in the synagogues, and he spoke with a leaping joy which made his
face like an angel's. This man was very dangerous.

In fear and anger his death for blasphemy was fixed. By ancient law he must be stoned. He was hustled out in the dark of the night, across the city to one of the hills. The Sanhedrin had no authority to carry out executions. Such a sentence broke the Jewish law which said that a man could not be condemned without a second hearing. It was fearful, huddled, and appropriate only for the dark.

The first witness against Stephen laid his hand on him, and toppled him over the cliff. The ancient law had many mercies and took into account many bitter ironies. The fall from the cliff was intended as a quick death. If the guilty man was not killed by the fall, then the whole community must bear the weight of his killing. The other witnesses, standing as surrogates to the whole, took off their clothes and laid them at the feet of the man who had toppled him over the cliff.

They stoned Stephen while he talked with God. At the last his voice rang in the darkness, "Lord, lay not this sin to their account!"

The young man who had toppled him over the cliff, at whose feet the executioners laid their clothes, was Saul of Tarsus, he who would become Paul the Apostle.

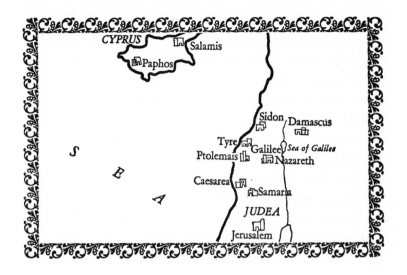

2

DAMASCUS
Release into Life

A Hebrew of the Hebrews, he called himself, *of the tribe of Benjamin, as touching the law a Pharisee; concerning zeal, an avenger of Judaism; touching the righteousness which is in the law, blameless.*

Paganism had built many bridgeheads into Judea through the cities of the Decapolis and along the Mediterranean coast of Palestine, where the people were half-Greek, half-Jewish, the language almost wholly Greek.

Even the Maccabees had not succeeded in wiping out Greek as the strong language of Jerusalem. Aramaic might be more pious but Greek was more useful. This Hellenization offered subtle temptations; it made orthodoxy more orthodox, but it also left windows onto the world. It also made many Jews of the Diaspora eager to prove that they were more pious than the Jews of Jerusalem.

There is a tradition that Saul was a member of the Sanhedrin; his zeal, brilliance, and orthodoxy recommends the possibility. If it were true, then he was married and a father, for the old rabbis assumed that law enforcers with commitments of love would lean toward mercy.

But whether he was a member of the Sanhedrin or not, we can assume that he was married, for what Hebrew of the Hebrews, what lover of the Mosaic law, would withhold himself from the obligation of marriage? Among the Jews celibacy had never been a virtue— unless one thinks of the Essenes, and they were Greek in spirit.

After the killing of Stephen, armed men fell upon the Nazarenes. While Stephen's body was being carried to a grave, homes were invaded, children terrified, men and women caught or sent flying for their lives. Only the twelve disciples were left untouched.

What did they think, twelve men standing in amazement as the hurricane veered around them? And what did they think when they were obliged to notice the young man who directed the death of the Nazarene community, the young man who entered one house after another with the Levitical guards, laid violent hands on men and women, and threw them into prison?

Such burning zeal can make a man look like an apocalyptic angel, can give him a kind of beauty *in extremis*. Before such an awful force the beholder can only search and search within his own soul for a reason. Fear is the simplest reason. The young man was afraid. What was his fear?—that the vast, topheavy, intricate, defensive structure of orthodoxy could not survive assaults from without? Or the fear that reverberations of Jesus would grow louder in the chambers of his soul? The Nazarenes had told over and over in Saul's hearing the remarkable news of hope and redemption. He knew it word for word; what his mind rejected his spirit must have stored in a rocky vault.

The Nazarenes were being flung like grain in all directions. They were planting the message of Jesus with a speed that would have been impossible without this intervention of Saul. The disciples in Jerusalem heard that Samaria was already accepting the word, and sent down Peter and John without delay. The word, in the mouths of the flying saints, was being carried to Egypt and Ethiopia, Asia Minor, Damascus, Cyprus, and the islands of Greece. Those who were Hellenists took the word home.

What if it had remained locked in Jerusalem? The disciples of Jerusalem must have thought with bitter humor that Saul had become an angel of God. But merciful men on the Sanhedrin were aghast. There seemed no end to the havoc he wrought. Even the High Priest may have shown alarm, for any civil stir brought the Daggermen into the crowds or the Roman soldiers into the streets. If this tiger could not be leashed, he must be driven into the wilderness.

The High Priest gave him letters of authority to seize the Nazarenes who had escaped to Damascus. The Romans gave him the right to extradite any Jewish malefactor who had escaped from Jerusalem. Let the tiger exhaust itself where it could do no harm.

The authority carried by Saul was reinforced by a great number of Temple guards, for many Nazarenes had fled to Damascus, and by a scribe to clarify the proceedings. The road to Damascus lay across the hills of Samaria and the rising meadows of Galilee, through rich wheat lands to Capernaum. The procession moved across the brown mountains with a slow thunder of hoofs. It had a rough majesty for it represented the might of the Temple. Ahead lay Mount Hermon, with its snowy peak, and below the Sea of Galilee and the wild mountains of Moab. The tawny upland led them straight toward Damascus, its orchards, its holy rivers, its formidable task, its extirpation of heresy. A man can only be made over when his entire being longs for light. Stephen had ringed him around with light as he died. "Lord, lay not this sin to their account." How can one measure such love?

This land was rooted in memories. Hills and valleys remembered the search for the one God and His will. It was a very ancient land, where the spirit stirred, where God was the soul of man. . . . *O Saul, Saul, you burdened beast, why do you kick against the pricks?*

A man so impassioned with the law as Saul, so hard and charged with intellect, so wonderstruck by weights and measures, could never be made over by a flood of reason—only by a blinding light.

The truth which is inherent to such a man—from his childhood, from before time—becomes without warning a light which fills the farthest corners of his soul and sets free his mind.

Saul fell onto his knees into that blaze of light. *The Lord shall be thine everlasting light and the days of thy mourning shall be ended.*

The others saw an extraordinary brightness in the air. They stood trembling. They also were the sons of the promise to whom God had, in time past, spoken in most direct ways.

Saul, Saul, why persecutest thou me?

Who art thou, Lord?

I am Jesus whom thou persecutest.

Lord, what wilt thou have me to do?

Arise, and go into the city, and it shall be told thee what thou must do.

As quiet as snow, as simple as the growth of grass.

When he stood up the light still filled his eyes so that he could not see. A man took his hand and led him to his camel.

In dismay and compassion they led him through the gates, ecclesiastical bureaucrats who had been asked to look into the blazing wonder of a soul. If they who had

seen a great light at noon were distraught and uncomprehending, how could this city guess what had passed
through its gates?

A sea change that would make over the world.

Saul was put in the care of a man named Judas who
lived in a street called Straight. From the hospitality
asked of Judas, one may assume that he was a ruler of
the synagogue to whom the High Priest's letters were
addressed.

Let us assume many other things: that Judas was a
compassionate man, that he consulted with the Jewish
community; that he waited for the moving of the
waters; that there was a great deal of awed coming and
going, for this event outreached the plans of men.

The Jews of the Diaspora had been able on the whole,
to maintain a courteous alienation from the political
tremors of Jerusalem. This world of the synagogues,
stretching wherever the Jews had gone, was self-respecting, humane; in the synagogues a religion without sacrifice was practiced, for the first time in the world. Only
in the Temple were sacrifices made. The Nazarenes who
had fled to escape the fury of this touching silent figure
were the coreligionists and kin of the Jews of these
synagogues.

No one knew what Saul thought. He neither ate nor
drank for three days; to fast was to pray. *It shall be told
thee what thou must do* to release your life, a life which
had been compelled on such a self-obliterating course.
He had heard over and over what the Nazarene taught:

I am come that they might have life and that they might have it more abundantly. . . . Blessed are they who do hunger and thirst after goodness for they shall be satisfied. . . . Love your enemies; bless them that curse you, do good to them that hate you, and pray for them which despitefully use you and persecute you.

All we know is that with his soul's eye Saul saw a man named Ananias coming to him in power and affection. Power and affection he surely needed to link him to the world again.

When every reasoned purpose of one's life is swept away and intellectual pride is laid low and a man left naked to the world, he must either live or die. If he chooses life it is never the life he led before. Courage is measured here, for the first step must be taken blindfolded.

Somewhere in his spirit must have been a transcendent joy and exaltation. The beating of great wings filled his mind. In light upon light is vision seen.

He was the center of concern and compassion, and tenderness reached him from all directions. When Stephen died Stephen had said, *Lay not this sin to their charge.* When Stephen's master died he said, *Father, forgive them for they know not what they do.* Such tenderness is a great wind sweeping through the inner chambers. *I am Jesus*—not the Christos of hope nor the Messiah waited for by the law, but the tender, the compassionate, the brother, the man, the beginning, the door, the hope.

All life is a miracle. Waiting for Ananias was a miracle. Ananias approaching the house was a miracle, for Ananias had protested when told by his vision to go to the house of Judas where he would find Saul of Tarsus on whom he would put his hand to restore his sight. *Lord, this man did much evil to thy saints in Jerusalem and has come here to do even worse.*

But the Jew who knows that God is One is forced to yield to an implacable logic: however winding the course, all roads lead to that One.

When Ananias entered the house and passed through the amazed and incredulous elders, he came straight to Saul and put his hands on him.

Brother Saul. . . . See and that seeing will be the spirit of God.

Ananias had been assured that this young man was a chosen vessel to carry the message of Jesus to the kings of the earth. Now Saul rose up and he saw again, saw all those about him and also all the things within himself.

Ananias was a need fulfilled, a strong grip of love linking him to his brothers. By tradition Ananias was one of the seventy disciples of Jesus, one of those who fled before Saul. He behaved as a man who is strong, humble, and loving. He offered this unhooded hawk to the Nazarenes, some of whom were undoubtedly nursing wounds inflicted by Saul. By Ananias' authority and love, they were able to sit down with the man who had tried to kill them.

Just as Ananias was Saul's necessity, and Saul the necessity of Ananias so that both might give up old bonds and chains, so Saul was the necessity of the

Nazarenes. They were obliged to test the very sinews of their faith: the love which is all.

Sharing their meal with him was not simply the breaking of bread. It was putting aside suspicions, cynicism, and fear, finding a truth deeper than courage—that is, a flawless love.

He was their challenge. Did they understand the requirements of a flawless love? Sitting at the table, withholding part of themselves, waiting, watching, they had to say, as Ananias had been able to do, *Brother Saul.*

When the lame beggar was healed by Peter at the Beautiful Gate, he must have become for a time the epitome of legs, walking, dancing, leaping, running to the glory of God. So a man from whose eyes the scales have fallen, for whom the veil of the Temple has been rent, the middle wall of partition broken down, must for a time become the epitome of absolute clarity; his truth, all truth, his love, all love, his power to see without limit.

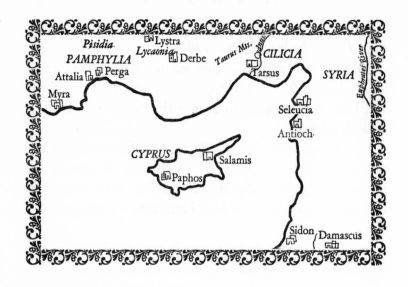

3

TARSUS
Lonely Years of Self-discovery

Perhaps Saul knew a complete peace for only a day and a night. Perhaps at the end of that time he saw himself through the eyes of others: to the Jews a traitor, to the Nazarenes unproved.

There is no comment on the feelings of the Levitical guards who had come from Jerusalem with Saul, we do not know what report they made to the High Priest. There is no indication what Judas thought, who had entertained both Saul and Ananias. And we have nothing

26

but our imagination to supply the response of the disciples.

But human beings are apt to match their actions to their experience. Bureaucrats must have taken a cold and harsh report back to Jerusalem, and the men who received it, being moved primarily by political wariness were, in all probability, shaken by outrage and considered expedient moves. As for Judas, he saw what he saw, and a compassionate man has wide seams to his understanding. The disciples praised God that the wilderness could blossom like the rose, then went about their business. Whether Saul was a true miracle had yet to be seen. It was enough to thank God that his sword had been put aside.

In *Galatians* Saul tells what he did. "I conferred not with flesh and blood." He knew that men's advice would be useless. He knew that who and what he had become could only be confirmed by truth, that the time for men's advice lay in the future. Each man's experience is his own in accordance with his own need. Peter had been reborn when he had seen the undying Jesus on the shores of Galilee. Saul had been reborn when he had seen the blazing truth.

Whatever is true of truth belongs to each man, and to all, for truth is indivisible.

Saul went into the desert. The desert is like the sea. It owes nothing to man. If a man can survive its illimitable waste he is friends with himself and his God. Here the truth is held as dear as is water.

Below Damascus, the Arabian desert stretched as far

south as Sinai, as far east as the Euphrates. It was the land of the Nabataeans, an Arab people whose capital was Petra. They controlled the great trade routes from the east across the desert, they carved dwellings, temples, and tombs out of the rosy rock, they built aqueducts and made the desert bloom as no one had ever done before.

Whether Saul stayed three years or forty days in desert villages or the waste wilderness concerns no one but himself. More imperative than hunger was the need to know the man within, to know and trust the Saul who in his deep struggle for the truth of being had fought so hard against it. He remained in the desert until the questions were answered.

Those who come under the power of the desert know that it leaves its austere beauty on everything. The sun and loneliness, the sands with their vivacious life, cleanses the body and mind till only the undiluted, the austere, the pure remain. The sky which has no touch of the finite wipes out forever certain assumptions of mortality.

When he returned to Damascus, Damascus became the mold which shaped his work.

Nazarenes had no churches. They had only their instructions, "Go ye into all the world and preach the gospel to every man. Heal the sick, raise the dead, cast out devils, freely ye have received, freely give."

Saul had the temerity to begin in the synagogues. He who had come with letters to the synagogues to extirpate the Way-seekers stood up now to speak in their name.

One wonders if he had any friends at all except Ananias.

A man whose eyes have been opened is freer than anyone else. But this also means that he sees, more clearly than ever before, what has been wrong in his life. He has still a monstrous burden of guilt to throw off, he has much absolute truth to exact from himself. After that there is no mystery of heaven and earth he must not be willing to learn; he is a stranger to no secret thing; he is a friend, most particularly, to the divinity within himself. The deepest wells of a man's spiritual insight must be uncovered.

Never before in the history of the world had men been assured they were loved, free, and deathless. This message of Jesus needed a new heart, a new tongue, a new mind.

The first time Paul rose in the synagogue to speak, he rose as a Jew subject to the discipline of the Law. He preached that God so loved man that he sent his son, Jesus the Christ, to redeem man through this love—but who could be expected to hear this remarkable message when all that reverberated were the stories of this Saul who had made havoc in Jerusalem and come to do the same in Damascus?

He talked of a Law of spirit uncorrupted by ceremonies, scribal interpretations, rabbinical logic. This was a blazing noonday truth which spoke to the heart. If it brought chaos to some, it brought the power of God to others. But as the Nazarenes began to see him without the glaze of fears, the orthodox began to harden their minds.

Saul must have known where the dangers to himself lay. He had known them in all their detail when he had invoked them against others. Although moderation was urged upon him by Ananias, let us say, who was by tradition a lawyer, Saul knew of no moderate ways to the truth. Through the monstrosity of his own experience he knew that each man must learn the truth for himself. There was no vicarious salvation.

Many years later Saul wrote, "of the Jews five times received I forty stripes save one." Why not in Damascus? The effrontery of the situation he created must have driven the devout to a fury. This man, who had betrayed the authority of the Temple, this apostate, this smart young fiddler of sacred dogma, was made to feel the lash of the law.

Forty blows not to be exceeded was the Mosaic punishment for betrayers of the Law. So that the punishers themselves did not break the law by miscount, thirty-nine were administered on the bare back.

A man is beaten and he rises up with commotion in his heart and his limbs in pain. What he does with that commotion and pain tells his story.

Saul himself had once exploited all the dangers which lay before the heterodox. He knew them one by one. He knew what to expect. Judging from his words and his actions, his candor, his relationships, nothing human was strange to him; his own imagination and sensibility, his own passion and reason, had carried him over the same ground. But there is no smell of a martyr about Saul. If it seems as though he went looking for trouble—

preaching in the synagogues, for example, or challenging
authority—what else could he do? The synagogue was
his home. The Nazarenes had never surrendered their
identity as Jews. The fierce punishment to which they
had been subjected was disciplinary action.

The synagogue was the cradle of subjective inspiration, its language was heard in the dialogue between God
and man; it was the magnet for those Greeks willing to
accept circumcision to confirm an ideal. So let us assume
Saul was beaten at this time—and that, shaken and humiliated, he staggered to his feet with a deeper understanding of what the Nazarene had endured and the
demands of the testaments of truth.

Any man who fooled himself that there was an easy
road through the world's shambles and fears was not fit
to put his hand to the plow.

Our knowledge of Saul in Damascus is a mass of conjecture. We do not even know how long he remained.
Three years is mentioned, but three years after his return
from the Arabian desert or three years from the time
of his vision is not clear. The work of the Nazarenes in
Damascus seems to have been independent of Jerusalem.
Autonomy appears to have been the practical ideal. Each
community was responsible for its good works and therefore its own good news.

Damascus was set in a paradise of fruit trees, between
barren mountains and a desert. Sometimes the *khanaseen*
blew for days over the city, and the sky became red with
flying sand. Trees bowed, and men walked bent in half,
with their mouths and noses covered.

Damascus was a violent city. It was called the oldest city in the world; it had had a long time to learn the full nature of evil. East of Damascus were Parthia and the desert tribes straining against Rome, north, Hellenized Asia both vigorous and corrupt, south the majesty of Palestine, west the Mediterranean world lashed to Rome. Damascus had fallen under the control of the Nabataean king, Aretas, though the Romans had never quite released their hold and would soon control it again, for Syria was a Roman province.

The fruit-vendor or the water-seller might be a Roman spy. Soothsayers, wandering actors, mendicant priests were often in fact Parthian, Jewish, or Persian spies or smugglers or desperate plotters. Bribes were as freely offered and accepted as the air.

This both increased the danger for Saul and gave him a protective coloration.

Whether the Temple authorities made any move against Saul is unknown. Certainly his apostasy was alarming, but shrewd minds would be reluctant to give him any opportunity for defending himself. Short of a political dagger in his back, there was no easy way to silence him. His teacher Gamaliel, who by virtue of his office held a moral authority over him, was a man of tolerance and his insights may have been too sensitive and subtle to demand an accounting.

All we do know is that at the end of three years, "the governor under Aretas the king kept the city of Damascenes with a garrison desirous to apprehend us." Had Saul offended the Arab king Aretas? Had Aretas a

reason for conciliating orthodox religionists? All we
know is that Saul received a warning; "and through a
window, in a basket, was I let down by the wall and
escaped his hands."

He walked—unless some countryman gave him a ride
—back to Jerusalem along the road he had ridden as a
man in the full panoply of authority.

Obviously he *chose* Jerusalem. He could have gone a
number of other places. But morally he could no longer
avoid the danger—the danger from the Temple and,
even more subtle, the danger from the disciples. The
disciples were the archstone of Nazarenes everywhere
and they had given no sign that he was trusted or accepted as one of them.

If they rejected him outright he would have to make
another place for himself, but Saul had spoken with God
many times; "he said unto me 'my grace is sufficient for
thee, for my strength is made perfect in weakness' . . .
I am become a fool in glory."

Jerusalem was the city which he knew spiritually and
topographically as he knew his own hand. But where did
he belong?

Did he have a wife and family? Did he return and
find them gone? Was the door to them shut by an authority against which he could not contend?

He made overtures to the disciples but he was re-
buffed. They said frankly that they were afraid of him.
They did not believe in his conversion.

There are no easy tokens by which to recognize a
newborn man.

Saul's refusal to be turned away is a remarkable part of this subtle and intricate man. It seems as though he knew himself better than anyone else could know him. He shook each experience till it yielded its fruit.

To prove himself and to unburden his spirit, Saul must have preached in the streets and the outer courts of the Temple, for it is hard to believe that he remained silent. It is hard to believe that he was not recognized. It is hard to believe that a plan was not made by the authorities to wipe him out in some fashion that would involve the community—as Stephen's death had involved all the people.

But a remarkable large-souled man (all of whose acts were larger than life) intervened as midnight was striking. He was named Joseph, a Jew, a Cypriote, a man of wealth who had sold some of his land and given the proceeds to the disciples as a token of the fellowship of sharing. The Nazarenes called him Barnabas, son of reconciliation.

He spoke to Saul, judged Saul, and brought him to Peter.

Time was wiped out.

Saul said later that he met only Peter and James, that he spent fifteen days with Peter. The intention to see no one else was apparently deliberate: Peter was by temperament and great heart the spokesman for the apostolic community which was still the seedbed of the church. James, as the brother of Jesus and by reason of his own piety, had acquired a singular position which no true courtesy could ignore.

Saul's revelation needed no confirmation. Its life was dependent on his own inner grace. But such an experience could remain abstract and vivid only to himself. Communication needed warm terms; contingencies had to be met. The hourly, daily, weekly retelling of Jesus' ministry would have warm and compelling answers for those contingencies. Nothing human had been alien to Jesus and nothing human would be strange to Saul.

On the other hand, the validity of revelation, the principle of grace, had to be acknowledged by the disciples, for as time went on, and the personal friends of Jesus' vanished, legends could not be allowed to turn a living power into a cult.

Peter gave him no rules, no formulas, no ceremonial directives, no pride of place. Would the world truly be faced in this free spirit, without plan? Saul also found something so simple and unworldly that he sensed a danger: the Way might remain such a modest bypath that it could be obliterated by the great highways of the world.

These disciples were good Jews bringing the good news to other Jews. James, the brother of Jesus, was allowed into the inner courts of the Temple where he knelt day after day praying for all the people. Soon the Nazarenes might be like the Essenes, exotic but familiar blossoms of Judaism.

To the disciples Jesus was the core and center of life. "But for me I cannot know him after the flesh." Saul and the disciples were both right. The passion of life which Peter communicated, what he had seen—Jesus walking and talking, a master of men, making the heart burn—was mixed in a warm and nourishing pottage to be served under the Palestinian sun.

The passion of light seen by Saul, brighter than the noonday sun, illuminating the very nature of life without the limitations of time or death, was like a river, breaking down partitions within the rooms of a man's soul, carrying the place where he dwelt on its crest.

The warm communal sense created by the disciples—all peasants, all simple, homely men—gave more to Saul perhaps than he gave to them. For the intellectual man has much to learn from the tenderness of life, and no doubt Saul needed such a warm centering in this city where cold legality had distinguished his life before.

Those who had been his friends and supporters—priests, rabbis, Pharisees, Sadducees—were now his enemies. Those whom he had persecuted in time past, hearing of his days with Peter, glorified God but remained watchful.

In *Acts* it is said he roused the hellenist Jews to plot against him. In *Galatians,* Saul says nothing of the kind. He merely says he went on, into Syria and Cilicia.

However, Saul had a vision while kneeling in the Temple. His capacity for seeing with fresh eyes, hearing with fresh ears, being willing to credit more in heaven and earth than could be explained with the dull senses, is perhaps the greatest miracle about Saul. He who had lived by his intellect, who had been so burdened by the density of reason, was able to leave it as finally as a

chicken leaves its shell. Kneeling in the Temple, he saw
the familiar light from the Damascus road and heard it
speak, " 'Get thee quickly out of Jerusalem for they
will not receive thy testimony concerning me.' And I
said, Lord they know that I imprisoned and beat in every
synagogue them that believed on thee, and when the
blood of Stephen thy witness was shed, I also was standing by and consenting unto his death. And he said unto
me, 'Depart; for I will send thee far hence unto the Gentiles.' "

Saul disappeared into Tarsus for four years or fourteen years: it is impossible to know. But how could those
years be anything but a period of sowing and reaping, of
doubts, assurances, of who, where, and what am I? Every
man of heart, mind, and spirit has his Tarsus.

Tarsians, returning from Jerusalem, would have been
men of preternatural reticence if they had not told the
story again and again of Saul the avenger who had gone
mad and joined the Nazarenes; Saul, son of a family
honored in city and synagogue.

Tarsus was to him a city unparalleled for learning the
topography of the future.

It had greater vitality than Athens, for two of the
chief trade routes united fifty miles east of Tarsus and
came into the city as a single road. Of the university,
Strabo said that "the people of Tarsus have devoted
themselves so eagerly not only to philosophy but also to
the whole round of education in general that they have
surpassed Athens, Alexandria, or any other place that

can be named where there have been schools and lectures of philosophers."

Perhaps we do, in fact, know pages and pages of Saul's life in Tarsus, for his skill with the Athenians may have been a pale copy of his skill with the Tarsians, his patience, sharpness, and despair with the Corinthians and Ephesians a translation of his experience with the Tarsians.

As a boy this city had been his nursery. Now, where the great trade routes met, stood Saul, the man who would become master of market places and road junctions. Saul wrote that he was five times beaten in the synagogues, three times beaten by the Romans, once stoned, three times shipwrecked, a night and a day adrift on the sea, "in perils of water, in perils of robbers, in perils by mine own countrymen, in perils by the heathen, in perils in the city, in perils in the wilderness, in perils in the sea."

Three shipwrecks are incontrovertible experiences. The journeys by sea which are spoken of in *Acts*—from Antioch to Cyprus, from Cyprus to Attalia and back to Antioch, from Troas to Philippi, from Corinth to Ephesus to Syria are recorded with careful detail and no mention of shipwreck. But in these lost years what might not have happened?

"Going into the regions round about Syria and Cilicia" was a compass circling wide. Syria and Cilicia may have been his radiant point from which he moved as the spirit led him. And wherever he went in this Mediterranean world perils would have awaited him.

Although Roman peace controlled pirates at sea and brigands along the great Roman roads, its authority did not venture into the lesser roads or up the lonely scarps of the mountains where desperate men robbed for a penny.

The Romans had set inns at regular intervals where relays of horses, food, beds, and prostitutes waited. But they waited only for travelers with an official diploma or permit. In crowded and filthy wayside khans, the foot-traveler slept on the ground, starved or ate according to his means, and was ritualistically robbed.

Saul left no legends. He did not attempt to establish communities—unless the churches he addressed later in Phrygia, Lycaonia, Cappadocia were the fruit of these years, or the churches in the Greek cities along the coast: Ptolemais, Tyre, Sidon. The hint in *Acts* (27:9) may be a perfectly valid indication that he knew the coast of Crete and knew why Fair Havens was a satisfactory place to winter.

He was an itinerant holy man, and this Asian world was dusty with such men. During these years he grew into his own "stature of manhood in Christ Jesus." He observed, learned, and taught. He may have seen how wise it was to put a line between himself and the peripatetic holy men: to be self-supporting, to give, not beg as they did, to make sure that his clothes were clean and well ordered. Otherwise the thousand cults of the east could in their timeless, unhurried way blur his distinction and absorb his message without a trace left.

Saul took to the roads in heat and rain, speaking with his own authority about a vision which belonged to him. He built no heroic legends of Jesus, for none are associated with his teachings at any time. He did not call on the words of Jesus to support his own inspiration. His teaching was a spiritual assessment of Jesus' ministry. His message was based on love and freedom as revealed by the Christ. Never before had the world been told that love and freedom were men's natural right.

He learned during these lonely years that a man must be obedient to his own spiritual insight or lose his power. Memorabilia of Jesus would never have cut to the joints and marrow of a man's being as did his own vision of the Christ.

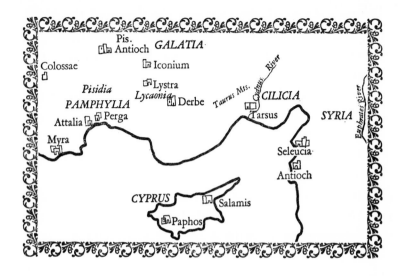

4

ANTIOCH
Center of the Compass

These years were vivid and imperative, although we have nothing but probabilities to support this statement. But men and women with Greek and Jewish and Roman names were spreading the word of a new hope in the world as far as Rome, as far as the northern steppes.

The journeys had begun with the seventy whom Jesus had sent out. When Stephen was killed and Saul fell on the Nazarene community in Jerusalem the circumference widened still farther. Hellenist Jews escaped to their homes in Egypt, Libya, Cyrene, the shores of the Black Sea, Parthia, the Indian Ocean. The news of Jesus the Messiah was spilled on the Greek air and carried like spores.

Many years later, the epistles which carried Paul's name made references to primitive traditions in these early communities, but the community in Syrian Antioch is as close as we can come to a knowledge of such early groups.

In Antioch was Symeon who was called Niger and this means "black" which might mean "Africa," Lucius of Cyrene, a man with a Roman name and a North African home, and Manaen who bore a complimentary title which indicated that he had been a playfellow of a prince, Herod the Tetrarch. These men were Jewish Nazarenes. The Jewish colony in Antioch was large and prosperous with many synagogues and with full civil rights.

At first these Nazarenes talked only to the synagogues, for Jesus had been a Jew sent to the Jews. But the emancipation which came with being Nazarenes made them listen when brethren from Cyrene and Cyprus came to Antioch flaming with the conviction that the good news must be spread wherever there was a listening ear. The Antiochenes, vividly aware that they held great forces in their hands—forces more powerful than they could immediately define—must have regarded those Cypriotes and Cyrenians with love and attention. All, with one mind, turned to the "Grecians," those uncircumsized who stood on the fringes of the Hellenized synagogues not sure whether to come in or stay out. Their proselytizing was so swift and successful that the apostles in Jerusalem sent out Barnabas, that peripatetic, large-souled man, himself from Cyprus, to bring back to them honest word of incredible rumors. When he came to Antioch he "saw the grace of God and was glad . . . for he was a good man full of the holy spirit and of the faith. And he departed to Tarsus to seek Saul." This was probably in the year 45 A.D.

Many great men have been lost in the shadow of Saul. But not Barnabas. His generosity seemed without limits; his unfailing sense of what was needed by man or community had a large share of genius.

When he found Saul he brought him back where he was most needed.

Some of the Antiochenes had, in all probability, suffered at the hands of Saul. But these were old wounds which must be relinquished forever. In the intervening years his travels and his work in Syria and Cilicia and perhaps farther afield had become well known to them, so that when he came to Antioch he came as their equal in experience.

The impetus of the work in Antioch, spilling over the city into the countryside, needed the widest experience and the most tireless skill.

Four or ten or fourteen years of his own ministry had made Saul master of trial-and-error, confirmed his wide humane resources, but left him, for all we know, a man committed to a solitary course of action. Barnabas, knowing when the time had come for the lonely genius of Saul to be stretched to its widest extent, had had the temerity to claim him.

In Antioch Saul learned the power of this collective life where each individual was indispensable . . . "for the body is not one member but many," he wrote years later. "If the foot shall say, Because I am not the hand, I am not of the body: is it therefore not of the body? And if the ear shall say Because I am not the eye . . ."

And because he valued foot, eye, and ear, he became a part of the community at Antioch, teaching, preaching, and utilizing the wise man's prerogative to understand that "when one member suffer, all the members suffer, or when one member be honored all the members rejoice."

We can only assume that imagination and humanity determined the course of these communities wherever they grew. Disciples sent into the Syrian countryside— or farther, to Greek cities along the Lycian coast—were men of families who took their families with them. These disciples were not ascetics; these were men and women indistinguishable from the world they wished to proselytize except in their moral orderliness and their spiritual vision.

They were Jews, or else they were Greeks who had accepted Judaism. This meant that they were self-supporting, thrifty, carrying themselves with dignity, in deliberate contrast to the disheveled holy men of the East who made a virtue of poverty, dirt, and ecstatic speech. The Nazarenes of Antioch made it clear that they were not priests, for the colleges of the priests of Atargatis (who was also Astarte and Aphrodite) were in the country near Antioch, and the eunuch priests filled the roads, carrying the image of their goddess, balanced on forlorn donkeys, from town to town. The priests were often old men, heavily rouged, with painted eyes, who chanted and whined the glories of Atargatis like tireless old birds, beat drums and cymbals, danced, leaped, pranced, and when a crowd was attending, slashed their bodies as they whirled in a dance until the onlookers were splashed with blood and shrieked with them in frenzy.

The Jews must have reflected wryly that such priests and such deities had plagued Moses and Ezekial, Jeremiah and Hosea; their durability was remarkable. The only difference lay in the fact that Roman statecraft now supported them with money.

As for Antioch itself, here was a formidable challenge.

In every city human nature was fundamental and inexorable. In every city the gloss of education, superstition, and indigenous ways had to be taken into account. In Antioch the heart of the people lay in a relentless pursuit of pleasure. Pleasure was the city's pride and purpose. Antioch promised every gratification.

The educated and well-born were Hellenized; the free workers were Asian, the slaves came from every place under the sun. It was oriental in its voluptuousness, Greek in its language, Roman in its position in the world: the legate of Cilicia and Syria who ruled Palestine had his seat in Antioch.

It was second only to Alexandria and Athens in its greatness and beauty. Sheltered by black and splintered mountains on all sides but the sea, its valleys were filled with fruit trees and vines, and flowers grew on the hills.

Because it was beautiful and salubrious it had been fashionable since the days of the Seleucid kings—Alexander's heirs—and the Caesars had added to its splendor. They had built marble palaces and theatres and circuses and amphitheatres, put up statues to all the gods, piped water to the houses, and laid down the great Roman road of squared stones that crossed the land. Herod the Great had also paved with marble two and a half miles through the city and lined this marble road with a colonnade of colored stones under which the Antiochenes could walk in the shade.

It was the city of Adonis whose festival of death and resurrection was celebrated in the heat of the summer. It was also the city of Aphrodite and of the river-god Peneus whose daughter Daphne had been loved by Apollo. The groves of Daphne lay for ten miles along the banks of the Orontes and within these groves the worship of Aphrodite took such orgiastic form that Roman soldiers were forbidden to enter.

It was also a city filled with constant perfume so that the senses were satiated, and a city given over to perpetual light. When the dark came, the circuses and theatres and race courses were bathed in floods of light, and the streets were lighted by thousands of torches and by lamps fixed to the buildings. It seemed as though Antioch was attempting to thrust back death rather than to seek out life. Brooding over the city was a great carven head of Charon, god of death, wearing a golden crown. It had been cut into a crag of Mount Silpius by a Seleucid king who had hoped to avert a plague by proving that Death already ruled the city.

One could see the monstrous head with its golden crown from every part of the city. What happens to people when their lives are so governed by death?

Saul must have seen the great brooding head every day that he lived in Antioch.

The very heart of Saul's message was the triumph of life: O, *death where is thy sting? O, grave where is thy victory?*

The passionate license of this city which loved every sensation forced the men of the Nazarene community to become shapers and improvisers of moral good, prophets and teachers, sowers of hopeful crops, reapers of whatever grew, mothers and fathers of spiritual infants.

The air was filled with the subtle beguilements of ancient superstitions and Greek mystery cults. Some of the Greek mystery was profoundly noble, offering a vision and a purgation. It translated into words and secret acts the deepest intuitions of the human spirit. Death and resurrection lay at its heart. The seed of the Great Mother, dying in the ground to become the growing corn, was the essence of universal hope, held against all the testimony of the senses.

But even the noblest mysteries were drenched in blood. The mystery of Cybele was fulfilled when the initiate was put naked in a pit over which a bull was sacrificed. Its blood, pouring over the initiate, proved that life was

unconquerable. Mithras, the sun god, whose worship
became the special cult of Roman soldiers and the
official rival of Christianity in the years to come, also
initiated his followers in a pit over which a bull was
sacrificed. And in the Orphic brotherhood, the purified
drank the blood of a sacrificed bull to prove his union
with a dying and resurrected savior.

But all these cults were dependent on something so
ambiguous, so capricious, that hope was infinitely frail.
The gods were not anxious that men should be godlike.
If they occasionally gave a blessing to men, they would
as swiftly take it away. Man's only destiny was to learn
the nature of his helplessness. His sublimest hope was to
bear his helplessness with fortitude and dignity.

Who could bear the weight of being man unless
savior-gods, like Attis, Tammuz, Adonis, Dionysos, Orpheus, who died and lived again, gave some token of a
future? Unless the creature, man, could believe that the
seed which died in the ground was reborn in the growing
corn, that man endured through his son, that night was
succeeded by day, his reason for existence was cancelled
by the idiocy of the human condition.

The Nazarenes, born into the same need, preached a
substantial hope, a steadfast understanding that man was
not a helpless victim, for the Cause of the universe was
Spirit, Truth, and Love, a conscious force which gave
purpose to all living things as "God is not God of the
dead but of the living."

Most listeners heard only one thing—that they were
loved, that hope was substantial, that Jesus had shown

the way to life. They saw sickness vanish, the confusion of sin wiped out, death tendered sterile. Many were amazed that no initiation fee was required for this mystery, no priests demanded placation, no sacrifices were offered. The men of Jesus observed how often tears were the response to their words, tears of relief perhaps that the fearful ambiguities of life were for a moment shattered.

The seekers brought as little or as much of themselves as they could spare. Some brought husbands, wives, children, brothers, mothers, fathers, friends. Some brought nothing for they had nothing to bring.

The Nazarenes found that if their own hands were blackened by toil they were heard even more readily. When they said that each man was a law to himself to choose the good and refuse the evil, slaves and women wept for joy, for they were the most bound, most hopeless.

A "church" was not a place of walls and roof; it was the word falling onto the good ground, the seed taking root. It was whatever place or time a Saul, a Barnabas, a Symeon, a Lucius found himself with a listener. A church was a street where the message of hope contended with a frenzied Syrian crowd or it was a friend's house where all sat down together to share a meal. Jew and Gentile, slave and free, men and women broke immemorial barriers. Some learned to give the kiss of brotherhood without delay and find their own in another's good; but some rich men were afraid even within their riches. Each learned, in fear or joy, that he must work out his own salvation since there was no vicarious illumination.

For the Jews who came to the Nazarenes, this sitting down to eat with the Gentiles was the demand which put the heaviest burden on them. It violated the Mosaic code, it struck at the very root of their integrity as Jews. Their separateness had alone preserved them against the voracious moral filth of the pagan world. Yet, how can a man, commanded to love, draw a line and say, "This side is for you and that side is for me?"

It was a measure of love that each gave up a treasure to gain a richer truth.

In Antioch the Nazarenes were first called Christians.

Antiochenes were great mockers and lovers of political epithets. *Chrestus* sounded to them like a party leader, so they called *Chrestiani! Chrestiani!* after the preachers and teachers until the shout became a convenient and ironic designation. It had little meaning for the men of Jesus who scarcely ever used it. The names they called themselves had for them greater meaning: brothers, saints (that is, consecrated), Way-seekers, believers, servants and slaves of Christ. Yet the derisive Antiochenes were the instruments of a new wisdom. *Little Christs*—each man responsible for his own soul.

Peace in Judea was more elusive than ever. The country had been in a mounting crisis for ten years. The Herodians had quarreled over their tetrarchies and carried their quarrels to Rome. Caligula had given Agrippa the title of king which had roused the anger of Agrippa's brother, Herod the Tetrarch, who for his

protests was sent into exile in Spain. This turned the
eyes of Caligula toward Judea, and in his megalomania he
determined to have himself hailed as a god in the Temple
at Jerusalem.

Petronius the Roman legate in Syrian Antioch set out
with two legions to raise the sanctuary statues to Caligula. He carried orders to put to death any resisters and
to sell the nation into slavery if the protests mounted.
He came as far as the sea port of Ptolemais. There he
found Jews and their families assembled in the plain
to implore him to respect the God of Israel.

Petronius was a cynical and civilized man. He sat
down with the Jews to reason the course of madness. If
he yielded to them, he would be put to death and another sent to impose the emperor's will. Every subject
nation had put up statues to the emperor-god; would
the Jews go to war against Caesar for a lonely recalci-
trance?

As an answer the Jews said they offered themselves,
their wives and children as living sacrifices. "These words
filled Petronius with astonishment and pity," Josephus
wrote. He hesitated. He called together the Herodian
aristocracy and the party of the High Priest in private
conferences; he held public meetings with the people. He
entreated, threatened, cajoled. It was the time of sowing
and no man would go into the fields; the life of the country had come to a halt. At last he said he would risk his
life by an appeal to Caesar.

Caligula replied by signing the death warrant of
Petronius, but a storm at sea delayed the vessel with the

warrant and Caligula died in time to spare both the legate and the Temple.

Agrippa who had spent his youth and manhood in Rome as an intimate friend of the Caesars found himself the linchpin in the plan to make Claudius emperor.

For this reason Agrippa was made king not only of the tetrarchies but of principalities which even Herod the Great had not ruled. Agrippa came to Jerusalem with great haste, determined to exceed all other men in his piety. He went daily to the Temple, observed all rites, and considered the ways he could endear himself to these remarkable people who had, by argument alone, stopped two legions of Rome.

He knew that the Daggermen were more inclined to his death than the Romans, and to demonstrate his patriotic zeal he turned his attention to that pacific cult, the Nazarenes. The Nazarenes were now large enough to tempt a king. Although observing Jews they had, through Peter's vision that all men were equal, sat down to meals with the uncircumcized. The king laid violent hands on them, seized James, the son of Zebedee, and had him put to death.

When Herod saw how well it pleased those whom he wished to please he seized Peter also.

One can assume that Peter was an uncommon man, made larger by life than Herod could ever understand. But Herod understood enough to see that Peter was well chained in prison. A squad of soldiers guarded him through every watch. When the Passover was finished Herod planned to turn him over to the crowds.

But clamorous prayer was made to God for him. Men and mountains have been moved by such means. God is as proper a word as any other, and economic in its forcefulness, to explain the effects which men call miracles. All cause is God and all consequence, and blessed are the pure in heart, for they shall see cause and effect as God.

Peter, sleeping, bound to two soldiers, had his way illuminated by a great light, and he escaped through the labyrinth of the prison into the black streets. As a sensible man who sensibly encompassed a vision he came to the house of Mary the mother of John Mark and knocked on the door. By tradition this was the house in which the last supper was held. Peter did not know that the Nazarenes were gathered inside praying for him. When the maidservant came, she was so overcome by this answered prayer that she left him standing outside while she ran to cry out the glad news. Poor Peter continued to pound for a long time, since his friends seemed reluctant to believe the power of their own faith.

Herod put to death the sentries, and then went down to Caesarea, for trouble had broken out in Tyre and Sidon. In Caesarea he arrayed himself in full panoply— robes entirely of silver according to Josephus—and sat on his throne in the theatre to harangue the people.

The people called him the divine Herod who spoke with the voice of a god, but as they were deifying him Herod saw a harbinger of his own mortality—he saw an owl sitting on a canopy of the theatre. All his life he had been told that an owl would foretell his death. So he cried out and his stomach became like white-hot flames, and in five days he was dead.

Agrippa's son was too young to rule, and Claudius put Judea once more under a procurator.

Men as experienced as those who led the church in Antioch—for none were simple men, they all lived in a world of intricate forces—must have known that the violent actions of Herod, and his own violent death, were not movements *in vacuo*. The Herods never moved except as a political expedient. Any experienced man could infer from this that the Christians represented some form of political catalyst, that they, with their Messiah, had become trope and metaphor of unease within the empire. To themselves they were very small eddies, but to Rome the Christians were Jews and the Jews were the most relentless stirrers of mischief and seekers of liberty within the empire. Without Jews and their damned love of freedom, the Roman force would rule everywhere.

In a world boiling with unrest, quickened with spies, leavened by the future, buttressed by the past, where Roman might was moving even against the Epicurean and Stoic philosophers who gave lip service to brotherhood and equality, the Antiochene Christians were obliged to face the indisputable fact that their challenge to the world must have the wisdom of serpents and the inoffensiveness of doves.

Yet could love and brotherhood be inoffensive?

It could split the empire from top to bottom.

If their miracles were mere wonder-workings they

would fail. If the miracles were instead the expression of
a love so deep and inherent in Truth that it transformed
the bones and sinews, then the Christians stood only a
little lower than the angels.

Never had men been offered such a hope before.

It challenged every power and every high thing that
exalted itself against the knowledge of God.

At some time they must have asked Elisha's question:
"What hast thou in thy storehouse?"

They had Jewish discipline, Greek curiosity and mag-
nanimity, Roman peace, highways and seas cleared of
robbers and pirates, Roman citizenship for many which
could protect them from sudden seizures, crucifixion or
scourging.

Above all they had Jesus' words, *Go ye into all the
world and preach the gospel to every creature. Heal the
sick. Raise the dead. Freely ye have received, freely give.*
They had the Christ-power to stand fast.

Now and then they may have looked back wistfully
at those dear simple days when they had talked only of
Jesus and had a handful of brothers to love. Dear, simple
days, broken to pieces by Saul the avenger.

Everywhere men and women were groping in the
dark, living in a world of imminent slavery, longing for
the end of portents and superstitions, trying to control
their fate by mysterious rituals: the reading of auguries,
the sacrifice of dumb beasts, ecstatic divinations, placation of dark gods, resignation, and terror.

It may be that the Christians spent a large measure of
their time smashing little idols, breaking amulets, show-

ing a lively scorn of auguries, for an air murky with fears
and incantations had to be cleared before their own
works could be seen. Street corner fakirs would not care
for this, and might raise a mob. Then constables with
their whips would beat all alike.

The Antiochene Christians stood at the center of a
circle; each direction was equal. They stood also at the
center of change. History demanded them. Everything
that had happened to them in the last fifteen years and
everything that was happening in the world, and above
all, the nature of the gift they held in their hands, thrust
them into the changing rush of time.

No man could be left out.

The Antiochene Christians waited only to be told in
which direction to move. When the "Spirit spoke to
them" it was clear that Barnabas and Saul must proceed
to the "work whereunto I have called them" in Cyprus.

Barnabas, Saul, and John Mark set out.

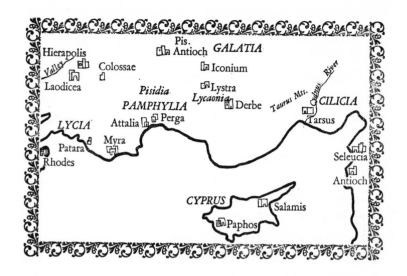

Hierapolis Pis. Antioch *GALATIA*
Laodicea Colossae Iconium
Pisidia Lystra
PAMPHYLIA *Lycaonia* Derbe *Taurus Mss.* *CILICIA*
LYCIA Attalia Perga Tarsus
Patara Myra Seleucia
Rhodes Antioch
CYPRUS Salamis
Paphos

5

CYPRUS & PERGA
He Ceases to Be Saul

Travel and movement were endemic to this age. "Many people," Seneca wrote, "make long voyages to see some remote sight." Plutarch was enthralled by the "globe-trotters who spend the best part of their lives in inns and on boats." All harbors and seas were bright with sails, "more peopled than the land," Juvenal said.

The Romans had made this possible with their great consular roads which ran across plains, mountains, and rivers. At regular intervals on these roads seats were provided for foot-travelers. Post stations stood every ten miles where fresh horses waited, inns every thirty miles.

True, innkeepers still robbed, brigands still waited in the mountains, seas were uncharted, Roman roads touched only a fraction of the land, but a climate of great expectation made the trackless wastes seem accessible and gave men a fresh yearning.

Cyprus was a green and purple island rising in mountains from the Mediterranean. Its name came from the copper which filled its mountains. From this copper the breastplate of Agamemnon had been hammered into shape. Cyprus was a very ancient island inhabited at the dawn of history, colonized by the Phoenicians, seized by the Romans, and made into a proconsular state.

Barnabas, Saul, and John Mark, coming across the sea from Seleucia, preached without delay in the synagogue at Salamis which was the chief port and the center of the salt mines. The island lay stretched before them, beautiful along the coast where the fishermen had their pillars of worship to Poseidon; beautiful in the mist-filled valleys where farms and vineyards lay, orange and olive groves, orchards of pomegranates; harsh and terrible along the mountainous spine and the broken mouths of the copper mines. The prosperity of Cyprus depended on these mines and on the great festival of Aphrodisea which drew thousands of pilgrims from all over the world.

This Cypriote Aphrodite held a power equaled only by Artemis at Ephesus. Both were fearful barbaric forces. The Cypriote Venus was the synthesis of all fertility worship: she was Astarte, Atargatis, Cybele. Her lover, Tammuz, Attis, Adonis, was forever killed and reborn. Her cult image was a blackened stone which had fallen from the sky, phallic in shape, burned and pitted on the surface. Under all her guises she was a remorseless power of nature whom kings had placated and women worshipped for a thousand years. As time went on, legend softened her into a goddess born of the foam, brought by the waves to the shores of Cyprus, but this insubstantial effervescence did not induce the same trust as did the pitted and terrible stone.

Her temple lay ten miles south of the capital of Paphos, and those miles were heavy with incense. Only male animals were sacrificed to this goddess whose altar was open to the sky—though no rain had ever touched it nor any blood left a stain. Her priestesses were holy prostitutes, and women pilgrims gained great merit by offering themselves to strangers and surrendering the money earned in this fashion to the temple.

It was a voluptuous and drugged air through which Barnabas, Saul, and John Mark made their way and it was protected at every step by superstition, self-interest, and fear.

If Barnabas, Saul, and John Mark spoke to farmers or fishermen or miners, there is no record. Their destination was Paphos, the administrative center and the seat of the Proconsul, and in Paphos, "they came upon a certain magician, a Jewish false prophet, named Bar-Jesus."

Bar-Jesus was a member of the Proconsul's household. The Proconsul was named Sergius Paulus.

Many high Roman officials demonstrated the eclectic nature of the empire by having priests of the great religions close to them at all times. This gave Rome an intimate benefit from all her conquests. Officials also depended on private seers, augurs, and astrologers whose task was to foresee and foretell events.

Magic and thaumaturgy were as much a part of this world as the growing of crops. The power of the magi had long ago spilled over its Persian border and assumed place and dignity in the Graeco-Roman world. A subtle infusion and reconciliation had even invested Judaic thought; there were mystery cults identified with the Yahweh-Sabaoth "the Lord of Hosts" and a Jewish image may have become a part of the esoteric Judaism which had been learned in Persia during the Exile.

Magic and magi had, indeed, a breadth of meaning. A magus could be a man of science, for science itself was a mixture of esoteric and empiric knowledge. Magi charted the skies, experimented with fire, earth, air, and water. Magi unlocked the secrets of biology and chemistry, were masters of knowledge and superstition. A man of science had to learn the dexterity of a street charlatan, not only because he wished to expose the tricks practiced on the gullible but because the line of demarcation between the occult and the explicable was a hair's breadth.

How the Jewish magus and the Jewish Christians met

is not clear. Bar-Jesus in his role of professional skeptic may have roused the curiosity of his master, the Proconsul, and thus invited a quick response from a lively man. Who was this Sergius Paulus? Pliny speaks of a Sergius Paulus as author of a book on Cyprian lore. This appears to confirm the comment in *Acts* that he was "a man of an inquiring and open mind."

Such an eclectic seeker must have heard and heard again all the theocrasy of wandering holy men, Indians, Buddhists, Zoroastrians; listened to all the arcane muddle of those who rolled their eyes inward and fell into convulsions; considered all the intellectual shabbiness of the itinerant Stoics, Cynics, Sophists, and Epicureans whose great days were over.

We do not know whether his curiosity was unquenchable or whether his attention had been caught in some special manner. Or whether he had a natural sympathy for the monotheism of the Jews. In any event he summoned Barnabas and Saul to speak the "word of God."

The word of God that they spoke was of Jesus of Nazareth who gave his life as a ransom for many so that men might learn how to love—how to heal the sick, bind up the broken-hearted, preach deliverance to the captives and life everlasting to all men.

Sergius was moved by this. Bar-Jesus was alarmed or, in a moment of intellectual mischief, he wished to pervert the simplicity of truth. Perhaps he challenged them in necromantic ways, perhaps he tried to empty their words by feats of magic. In any event he was filled with subtlety and devilishness so that Saul in the name of God demanded that he stop making crooked the straight paths of the Lord.

Saul foretold that he would not see the sun for a season, and immediately a mist and a darkness fell on Bar-Jesus.

There is a parabolic quality about this story which takes away some of the wretched black magic which is so unlike the clarity of Saul. *Blindness* and *seeing the light* were Saul's metaphors. They epitomized that transformation of being, the putting off of the old man for the new which was the heart of his revelation. *He had been blind but now he saw . . . Come out of the darkness into his marvelous light . . . In thy light shall we see light . . . whatsoever doth make manifest is light . . . ye are all the children of light . . . now we see through a glass darkly . . . but see, see.*

A man like Sergius Paulus would not have been moved to "believe" by a brutal act of magic. Yet he might very well have been moved by words filled with a light which blinded intellectual pretensions.

Bar-Jesus was filled with confusion and darkness.

Saul from this moment on takes the name of Paul.

There is no explanation why at this moment he ceased to be Saul. Saul was his Hebrew name; Paul was his cognomen as a Roman citizen.

It may heve been that this Proconsul, representing the might of Rome, represented also the vulnerability of Rome—the way Rome might be used and saved.

Or it may have been that the partition between Jew and Gentile dissolved in Paul at that moment and in all humility he saw himself as a man without home or tribe or city, surrendered to the world.

Cyprus was an island. It led nowhere. The roads of empire filled Paul's thoughts. Where they led Christ would go. The great cities of the trade routes would be the highway of the King of kings, the Shepherd of men who rejoiced to bring into his fold the halt, the blind, the righteous, the dispossessed, the great, the weak.

The moment when a man grows into his own stature of manhood appears in remarkable ways. Paul took command. He no longer followed.

They went north across the sea to Perga in Pamphylia.

From this time on Paul's destiny was as clear as the day. He moved without hesitation.

Perga lay away from both Antioch and Jerusalem.

It was nothing and nowhere in the large scheme of empire. A Roman provincial capital, custodian of the spear of Achilles, its great days were all in the past.

But above it, four thousand feet in the Taurus mountain, on the olive-clad Anthian plain, lay Pisidian Antioch, a Roman colony, a city standing at a great crossroads of empire where traders from the east met legates from Rome, and all races of men came together in a loose fraternity.

In the sluggish, malarial city of Perga Paul became ill (if one may draw this conclusion from his gratitude to the Galatians that they did not scorn and despise him in his physical condition).

Malarial seizures come without warning. Malaria can remain a thorn in the flesh for the rest of a man's life. Without warning, he can fall down in the street trembling as though possessed by a devil, his eyeballs starting from his head, his paroxysm so great that he can bite off his tongue.

In Perga John Mark refused to go on. No one knows why. John Mark was a kinsman of Barnabas and perhaps was jealous that Paul had taken command. But that is unlikely for there is no sign that Barnabas was jealous for himself. Perhaps John Mark, a youth raised in the heart of the apostolic community in Jerusalem, a spiritual son to Peter, was alarmed by this independent mission to the Phrygians, taken without consulting any authority. Perhaps he was reflecting a Jewish fear of the uncircumcized to whom they were turning.

Whatever the cause it brought anger and an emotion which, at the end of two years, opened a wide gulf between Paul and Barnabas.

At this time, however, Barnabas would not be separated from Paul. John Mark made his own way home and Paul and Barnabas set off on the dangerous journey which led them to Antioch in Pisidia-Phrygia.

The mountains began in a gentle way. In the spring they were filled with blossoms. The road they climbed was of rough marble. Here Bellerophon riding Pegasus had fought and killed the Chimaera but could not destroy her ghostly flame. It sprang out of the rocks near a temple to Hephaestus and could be seen, night and day, from the sea. Earthquakes had made great fissures which the cedars and junipers concealed as best they could. All through the hills small temples were crumbling into ruin and ancient tombs peered through the clinging trees.

The river Cestrus, narrowing through the gorges became here a torrent, and men and their animals died at the fords. On the peaks of the gorges were sanctuaries of Artemis, and in the tangles beside the road were marble or granite plinths which carried thanks for protection from death in the river or memorials to friends who had died at the hands of river or brigands.

Claudius Caesar had done all he could to make this road safe for travelers. New roads had been built up the gorges, armed patrols kept a watch, soldiers fought a continual battle against the runaway slaves and desperate old soldiers who became brigands. The patrols smoked the outlaws from the caves or sealed them into their caves, but still the dangers went on. No one in his right mind made this trip from Perga to Pisidian Antioch except in a large company. Even then, at twilight the dangers were immense. Brigands disguised by fearful masks fell on the travelers, maimed, robbed, and carried off children.

On journeyings often, in perils of waters, in perils of robbers, in perils in the wilderness, in weariness and painfulness, in hunger and thirst.

At length the road brought them into the volcanic Phrygian plain, four thousand feet above the sea. Here in the bright blue lakes of Linnai they could fish in the company of the wild cranes and reflect on a world at peace. Beyond the low range of snowy hills lay Pisidian Antioch in the Roman province of Galatia.

6

GALATIA
Of Liberty and Grace

Galatia was a wild majestic country lost in antiquity. These Pisidians, these mountain-dwellers, worshipped a huntress-deity guarded by a boar and a stag (whom the Greeks called Artemis out of courtesy). They also worshipped an unearthly horseman with a club who bore a resemblance to Hercules. Centuries before, Celtic tribes from Gaul had stormed over Macedonia, invaded the coast of Asia Minor and, forced on by the Greek kinglets on the Aegean, swarmed into the country of the mountains which soon took their name: Galatia.

The Gauls were blue-eyed, yellow-haired men who fought half-naked protected only by basket shields. As the years went on, their blue and yellow was, to a large extent, lost in the swarthy Hittites who for a thousand years had absorbed all intruders. Around Ancyra, Passinus, and Tavium, however, the blue eyes and the Celtic speech continued to dominate.

The Romans used the ruins of their fortified towns to build up their own bastions. By this time "Galatians" signified a heterogeneous people, for Greek colonists had been absorbed like the Gauls, and the local dialects of the dark mountain people had confused and reshaped the Greek tongue.

The Romans handled the Galatians deftly. When their conquest of the Greek orient was almost complete, Augustus proposed that Galatia pay submission to Rome and thus escape slavery. He gave to the Gaulish king Amyntas "the kingdom of Galatia," that is, Pisidia, Pamphylia, Lycaonia, part of Phrygia, and western Cilicia. Augustus' wisdom was demonstrated, for the kingdom passed back into his hands at the death of Amyntas, and became, with slight modifications, a province. Pisidian Antioch was given the status of colony.

A colony was a small piece of Rome. The *coloni* were Romans, usually Roman veterans brought from the West and settled in good fashion. The original colonists of Pisidian Antioch were, on the whole, soldiers of the

Alauda Legion who had served with Julius Caesar in Gaul.

The Galatians did not have the status of the *coloni*, but the new dignity which came to the city benefited them in many ways. Taxes were less heavy, and the attainment of citizenship was always a lively possibility.

The Romans were extraordinary masters of assimilation. By skillful use of citizenship, by translating crude local gods into members of the Roman pantheon, by recognizing dangers and neutralizing them, they held and extended their empire.

Only the Jews could not be swallowed alive, and so the Romans did the next best thing; they bound them securely in legal definitions which allowed the Romans control and the Jews autonomy. Every circumcized male was legally a Jew and, throughout the empire "the kingdom of the Jews within the city" confirmed their right to self-government.

A great aqueduct crossing the hills was the first view of Antioch. Standing here at the top of the world, Paul must have reached in his mind along that chain of Roman watchtowers, stretching east toward India, and stamped his foot against the great commercial highway which swung through Antioch to the cities on the Aegean.

These Pisidian Antiochenes had a reputation for being lively and dirty. They loved to ask questions and receive answers.

The Jews of Pisidian Antioch took on some of this inquiring air. Although careful to preserve their integrity, they were inviters. They held out their hands. Their synagogues had the reputation of welcoming the stranger, the Greek proselyte, any seeker of God. All looked for a hope, and here on the plateau of the world hope had a large meaning.

Paul and Barnabas (when they came into the synagogue one late summer day) were known to the rulers of the synagogue as rabbis, and were invited to take the seats assigned to honored strangers.

When the lessons for the day had been read the rulers invited them to "say on."

They spoke in Greek. What they said we do not know. Luke's long and rather dull speech in *Acts* has none of the fire which Paul's letter to the Galatians recalled to them: words which burned in their hearts. Perhaps on that first sabbath he spoke conventionally: "Men of Israel and those among you who feareth God, to you is the word of salvation sent." But on this day or another day he talked of liberty.

He addressed a world spiritually, politically, and morally enslaved. He gave the message that freedom was man's natural right because man was a whole being, capable of his own moral rectitude as a child of God.

In this world, shaped and buttressed by slavery, the liberty he proclaimed was more honored by a trembling in the heart than by any expectation of freedom. Slavery ruled everything.

In the Roman senate a proposal requiring slaves to

wear a special dress was defeated, for such a dress would merely prove that there were more slaves than free men in Rome. At any moment a man or woman or child could become a slave for a dozen reasons. Thus a slave might have a better education than a master. In addition to the slavery of men and women, bought and sold, were the categories of the freeborn with no rights of their own. Children were "enslaved" to their parents, who had the right of life and death over them. Women were chattels, helpless before the world if they had neither father, brother, husband, or male kin.

Humankind was divided into degrees of inferiority. In the synagogues proselytes, foreigners, wives, children, slaves did not have free and spontaneous access to God but had to be content with derived and qualified hope. The men of Israel thanked God each day that they were not slaves, children, or women.

It was Jesus who had first crossed this appalling chasm. He had taken children who had no worth, except to the heart, and raised them up as metaphors for the highest hope of man.

It was Paul who took women, slaves, and pagans and confirmed for them the statute of equality. "There is neither Jew nor Greek, there is neither bond nor free, there is neither male nor female, for we are all one in Christ Jesus."

This was an overturning of all the world's ways.

Paul said to the Galatians, "Where the spirit of the Lord is, there is liberty." This liberty delivered from the fear of evil; it made man responsible to his own life—

and this challenged Caesar. Paul turned them away from a god made in man's image and from the surrogates set up to explain him—and this challenged priest, magistrate, *and* Caesar.

To the Christian there was no Torah, no priestly intervention, no sacrifice, no mystic rites, no merit acquired by overt actions—only a man recognizing himself as the son and heir of God with all that this signified. Death put to death.

Not to *do,* but to *be* was the heart of his preaching. He demanded that Christians demonstrate a love which never failed. Love of Christ meant love of man, meant a profound sense of creation reconciled and unified. This was far more difficult than to sing praises or offer sacrifices or be bathed in the blood of a bull.

Paul rejected all authorities, institutions, customs, and laws as paths to the profound grace which revealed man as he was.

Grace . . . how Paul loved the word. The Galatians had gracefulness, graciousness, attractiveness, kindness, good will, gratitude opened before them. He used the words again and again. Grace had to him a transcendent quality because it was God's gift to man, spontaneous and irrevocable. Grace meant man new-made by an inner light, transformed by the "renewing of his mind."

Here was no vicarious salvation. Here was the grace of light, not sacrifice; faith, hope, and love were its components. To die with Christ meant to rise again free of enslavement to the fears and ills of the world, to live and move and have one's being in the power and grace of that Love which was God, to be the child and effect of divinity.

Paul used very few symbols to confound the symbols of the pagans who carried their cult images in all processions, but his language was rich in metaphors drawn from the world around him. The cross was his only symbol and it was a daring one in Galatia and all other places. To the Jews the cross was accursed; to the Romans it was the instrument by which criminals were executed; to the Greeks it had no meaning at all.

But Paul used this symbol of an accursed and cruel death for the purpose of proclaiming life. "For whatsoever a man soweth, that shall he also reap." If dying to the laws, traditions, and vagaries of the flesh was the only way to prove their lawlessness, then man found life indeed.

Paul did not set an easy path for those who heard him in the Galatian synagogue. It was the path which Jesus had set down when he said that a man must love his neighbor as himself. It was also the path set down by the great rabbis, but Paul went beyond rabbinical teachings, for he had no patience with abstract love or generalized good deeds. His neighbor's good was as important to him as his own, and relationships had a threefold power— mutual respect, help, and love. What he required was that a man know himself as God knew him, and this required a purity of heart and motive that must have made a new Christian long sometimes for the easy life of incense to Great Mother Cybele or obedience to minutiae of the law.

Paul was offering men not only the untrammeled hope and present expectation which Jesus the Christ had brought, but he was, in a manner incomparably daring, challenging the entire political and religious might of the empire.

Alexander the Great had insured his power in Asia by confirming and extending the oriental concept of ruler as surrogate god. Rome had, with great skill, extended this concept by making the Caesars divine. They permitted freedom to all religions if reverence to Caesar came first.

Paul was in effect striking at the foundation of imperial rule. This would cause more alarm to the Jews than to the Gentiles, for the Gentiles had no political freedom of any kind, whereas the Jews had the quasi-autonomy granted them by the Romans. This autonomy would be greatly jeopardized if the Christians (by Roman law a Jewish sect) roused Roman apprehensions.

As the weeks went on in Pisidian Antioch, and the stir created by Paul and Barnabas showed no signs of abating, the orthodox in the synagogue communicated their alarm to their more tolerant brothers. Their alarm was valid, for in a pagan world of sensuality and debasement the Jews had to fight an endless battle to maintain their high morality and ethics. Yet Barnabas and Paul talked of giving the pagans free access to the mercies of God, and required no assurances of good behavior save their faith. "Believe and thou shalt be saved." In the

Mosaic law, however, were set down the curses given to Moses by God, indispensable guerdons against the excesses of human nature. Did Paul and Barnabas know more than Moses?

Paul had to answer in a manner which went over and beyond a parochial question. If the pagans were not included in God's blessings, if men did not have free access to omnipotence, "then is our teaching vain and all else beside."

In everything he said or did Paul made clear his love of the pagans. The "passion week" of Attis for example might offend Paul, the Jew and Christian (when a pine tree in funeral cerements became a corpse and rose into new life at the end of three days), yet Paul saw this as a fumbling effort to see, through a glass darkly, the permanence of life. This inborn need was like a river which refuses to be confined between narrow banks of fear and breaks into new channels. The Christian task was to provide sure, new channels.

Since faith without works was dead, Paul and Barnabas required each man or woman who took the name of Christian to translate this meaning into his daily life. How well it was done depended on purity of intent and willingness to relinquish old ways of thinking. If the robe of Christ were indeed seamless, there could be no plucking at its threads. "For you have been called to freedom; only do not use your freedom as an opportunity for the flesh but through love serve one another. For the fruit of the Spirit is love, joy, peace, patience, kindness, goodness, faithfulness, gentleness, self-control: against such there is no law."

Then Paul honored the prophetic vision which had opened the way for this freedom. "If ye be Christ's, then are ye Abraham's seed and heirs according to the promise."

Such an overturning of the world's ways is most chilling to authority. Processions and mystic rites and esoteric knowledge and canons of law save a great wear-and-tear on the status quo.

Sometimes it seemed as though Paul detested the status quo more than anything else in the world.

As Sabbath succeeded Sabbath in Pisidian Antioch, the orthodox in the synagogue became even more deeply alarmed. They rose and challenged Paul chapter and verse. They threw against him the full weight of the law. Paul and Barnabas, standing in the midst of a multitude—"almost the whole city"—had to face and answer this orthodoxy so that the light would not go out in the faces of those who had seen a new hope—who "had received them as angels of God and were willing to give them their eyes." Paul and Barnabas answered boldly, speaking directly to the rigid and legal minds. Inspiration had been the genius of the Jews. For this reason "it was necessary that the word of God should first be spoken to you. But since you thrust it from you, and judge yourselves unworthy of eternal life, lo, we turn to the Gentiles."

And then they supported their boldness by a verse

from *Isaiah*: "I have set you to be a light for the Gentiles that you may bring salvation to the uttermost parts of the earth."

The pagans, the proselytes, some of the Jews, rejoiced with all their hearts and spread the word through the city and in the countryside, for in the distress and chaos of the world, where religion was cold or dishonest, where starvation and disease and authority had no mercy, they had been offered dignity and a hope.

Those fearful for their authority turned to legal action. It was a sad and sterile move because each legal act deepened a chasm, and in this chasm—in the centuries to come—many men would lose their lives.

The legal action had nothing to do with the Mosaic law. It was an invitation to the Romans to move against disturbers of the peace. Magistrates and wives of officials were invoked. Friends and neighbors, one might say, joined against the strangers who had brought dissension. The strangers found themselves blocked at every turn and forbidden to speak.

The disappointment of Paul and Barnabas must have been poignant, for Paul remembered it long and vividly. The relation of the synagogues to the city, the free intercourse, the spontaneous experiment in assimilated living practised in Pisidian Antioch, the warmth of their own reception, all these had raised their hopes for that ultimate desideratum—unity based on the indivisible nature of the Christ. In Pisidian Antioch Paul had called all men brothers and this was like a new birth.

But now the lictors moved in with their rods.

Paul and Barnabas shook the dust off their feet—a gesture of bitter irony: a pious Jew was careful not to carry home any dust from a pagan land.

They started down the road.

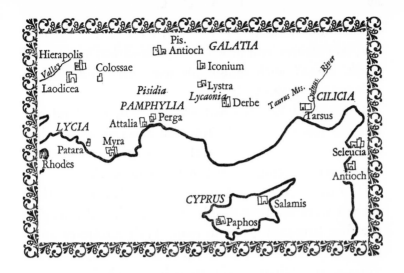

7

ICONIUM, LYSTRA, DERBE

Fools for Christ's Sake

The season was probably the autumn. The fall rains gave a freshness to the world, though the wild uplands through which they were passing were bleak, grand, and awful. They were known as the Treeless Region.

The road to Ephesus lay to the west, but they chose to cross the mountain pass and go eastward toward Iconium which lay eighty miles across this upland plain. It was a strange high desert world, where wells were scarce and the deepest in the land. It was exhilarating in

its loftiness, its incomparable sky, its intense benignant
sun, its vultures, and its eagles. The land was brown and
black, ringed with mountains with here and there a
volcano rising above the plain.

Greeks and Romans had passed across this land but
left few tokens. Even the Imperial Road on which they
walked was a narrow split in the brownness, a modest and
almost self-effacing symbol of the wide world.

The people who lived around the wells believed their
fathers were the first people of the earth and Phrygian
the first language given to man. Their antiquity ante-
dated Greece and Israel. When Athens and Sparta were
villages, this Hittite civilization had reached its power.
The signs of Hittite gods and inscriptions were all about
them, and the little gods and goddesses were the same
lewd figures with which Abraham had vied and Moses
had broken. The last foothold of those stubborn godlings
was here at the top of the world.

As holy men they would be welcomed and eat what
the villagers ate, cracked oats and sour milk and dibbis.
It is hard to think that Paul or Barnabas was silent; yet
it is hard to think what language they used.

Here there could be no question of being Jews among
Jews; they were obliged to be men among men.

They knew when they were approaching Iconium, for
an aqueduct spanned the hills and the country became
bright green from the river flowing out of the mountains. In the distance they saw the blue range which
separated them from Tarsus and the ruins of a treasure
house, built by Alexander, on a crag.

Iconium stood in a vast plain, almost as rich, and higher, than the plain on which Damascus stood. The city was so old that time itself seemed out of place. The Iconians said that when their good king Nannakos heard from an oracle that all the world would die when he died, he summoned his people to make "supplications with tears" and their weeping brought about the flood by which prophecy was fulfilled. No one was left in the world, and Prometheus recreated man here at this spot when he stole fire from heaven to give life to the images of clay which he had formed.

The Great Mother Cybele, come down from the high places around Pessinus, had ruled Phrygians and Lycaonians since the first seed had been planted.

Seleucid kings, heirs of Alexander, had tried to assimilate this ancient culture as well as to impose a Greek one. *Image-town* was the Greek genuflection to Iconium's unique position in the recreation of the world, and the Greeks readily accepted Perseus as the patron of the town (it was Perseus who had used the Gorgon head to turn into stone the enemies of Iconium), but they insisted that Athena, the greatest of their goddesses, must take precedence over Cybele.

In the end Cybele swallowed up Athena. How could Athena survive a goddess whom the Phrygians called "the mother who comes to help"?

Although the Romans now claimed all this land as theirs, and estates of the imperial family lay not far away, the Romans had made no impression and even Hellenism was a pale shadow in Iconium. Something

more ancient had already shaped the people—all but the
Jews, that is, who had crossed the mountains from Cilicia in the days after Alexander.

Paul and Barnabas went straight to the synagogue in
Iconium. The synagogue in Pisidian Antioch had driven
them away because they had touched too close to a
nerve, but they were men raised and trained by synagogues. Now they spoke in such a manner that a great
number of Jews and Gentiles believed.

From Paul there was always one message in multiplic-
ity: life without death, love without mutability, grace
as a gift of Christ, one body, one Spirit, one God and
Father of all who is above all and through all and in you
all.

Those who did not believe this doctrine were shocked.
They were many. The fixed authority that had acted
expeditiously in Antioch was lacking in Iconium. Here
Paul and Barnabas could only be expelled by the people
of the city. This took somewhat longer to accomplish.
In the palpable excitement that came from the signs and
wonders asked of them (a man restored in his heart, or
a child restored in its legs or a woman made over in her
hope), the city was divided.

This sense of stir, of a whole city tugging like men at
two ends of a rope, of life surging and of violence like a
molten flow was not duplicated again in Paul's experience until he came to Ephesus.

They remained in Iconium for a long time, speaking
boldly, working diligently to leave behind strongly
planted believers. When at length their enemies were

strong enough to mount an assault, they were warned and they fled.

"They fled," the Bible says, but they left behind every indication of returning.

They turned south to Lystra which lay six hours away in the broad Lycaonian plain over which rose the blue snowy mountains. Lystra stood on a hill, with gardens, greenness, springs, a lonely isolated town, speaking Greek and a crude dialect which could be scarcely understood. Yet this town of driftwood and backwater was on the Imperial Road, a *colonia* with a handful of Roman settlers, a fingerful of officials. It was the last link eastward in the chain of garrisons designed by Augustus to put an end to highway robbers.

The fierce little Isaurian mountaineers still swept into the town on their shaggy ponies, but their spirit of brigandry had been broken and they came in a spirit of wild trade and offered no dangers.

It was a place in which to wait until Paul and Barnabas could safely return to finish their harvesting in Iconium. There were few Jews, if any, in Lystra. Most of the inhabitants were Phrygians and Lycaonians. They worshipped ancient gods, spirits of the springs, hill deities, and an amalgam of Hercules, whom the Greeks of Lystra had invoked as patron of the city, and Zeus and Hermes, made city guardians because of a very old story in the countryside.

The ancients said that Zeus and Hermes had once appeared as hungry strangers to an old man and his wife in these hills. The old ones had shared their last meal in the name of holy hospitality. The gods had then revealed themselves and promised blessings without end.

It was a tender story and showed, perhaps, an element of expectation in the crudeness and isolation of Lystra that opened the way for the Christians.

Barnabas and Paul lost no time in speaking.

They spoke in Greek which would be well enough understood to translate into Lycaonian. They cajoled away fears, they made little jokes, they walked patiently beside these tossed and superstitious people. They talked to them plainly, and were apparently understood with equal simplicity—with perhaps too much simplicity, for the new Christians had to learn that the absolute faith required of them held no touch of magic and the new liberty held no license.

A lame man at the city gate heard the message with such intensity that Paul, recognizing the quality of his response, said to him suddenly, "Stand upright on your feet." The man leaped and walked.

Paul offered no terrifying exhortations as a priest would have done. He demanded no pay or sacrifice. The people set up a great cry, "The gods have come down to us in the likeness of men." Barnabas, quiet and large of stature, they called Zeus the chief god, and Paul who had given out the message they called Hermes.

Self-respecting men do not know how to act when they are called gods. The dialect of the people concealed the epiphany from them at first, but when the priests of Zeus, from the temple outside the gates, came to the place where the lame man had walked, and prepared to sacrifice to the Christians, Barnabas and Paul were filled with dismay.

They tore their clothes in the ritualistic protest of Jews against blasphemy. They ran among the people crying, "Men, why are you doing this? We are of the same nature as you. We have brought you the good news that you must turn from such vain sacrifices to a living God who made the heaven and the earth and the sea and all that is in them." They appealed to the people's own natural understanding of a divine power which was now being given shape and direction in order to lead them to the fullness of life.

It was only by concentrated and determined effort that they succeeded in establishing their humanhood.

All this might have plowed the ground for remarkable crops in Lystra, but their enemies, from Antioch and Iconium, followed them with a sick tenacity and roused the people.

Their enemies would have little appeal to make to the Phrygians or Lycaonians, but the Roman *coloni,* and the priest of Zeus who wore on his head the golden circlet of a state religion from which rose the heads of Roman emperors, would see the dangers.

Who stoned Paul? The Pisidian Antiochenes for blasphemy, or the colonists for the dangers he had raised? The stoning knocked him to the ground, and he was dragged out of the city and left for dead.

But he got up and he came back into the city and no

one dared to touch him except the lictors. As Roman officials they beat him dutifully for disturbing the peace and ordered him to leave the city.

"We are fools for Christ's sake . . . we hunger and thirst, are naked and buffeted, and have no certain dwelling place; and labor, working with our hands: being reviled we bless; being persecuted we suffer it."

The next day Paul and Barnabas set out for Derbe on the southeastern edge of the plain.

The hills were remnants of old volcanoes. The earth had shaken them into great pillars and caves, and, in days long out of memory, men had carved figures of the gods on their blue-black sides.

Straight before them was the massive blue range of the Taurus. Derbe was a military outpost, a trading center, a customs post, for the road to the Mediterranean lay over the mountains.

A synagogue was in Derbe. It may have been like many country synagogues, made up of simple men and women who stood together and were naturally responsive to a message shorn of legalisms. Derbe was an oasis. Paul and Barnabas preached, they taught, they were undisturbed. Cicero, when Proconsul in Cilicia, said sourly that there were not enough derogatory terms to describe the rustic Derbeans, but Paul and Barnabas were not homesick Romans. They planted well and the fruits grew as they watched.

They did not often have a chance to leave a town in peace. Derbe gave them confidence. The passes over the mountains into Taurus and the Mediterranean were closed by snow, so, without fear, they went back the way they had come, to Lystra, to Iconium, to Pisidian Antioch, nowhere harassed, confirming the men and women they had already blessed, urging them strongly to continue in the faith and not be dismayed by hard times or persecution.

They confirmed the loose society known as a Christian community: Christians would meet together wherever there was a welcoming roof. They would teach each other, the stronger—the elders—bearing the weak. Men and women would speak as the spirit moved them. Each must live for the other "in bonds of perfectness." Help, heal, speak the word of Love wherever a listening ear could be found.

Paul and Barnabas came to Pisidian Antioch and found that those who had held firm were now strongly rooted and prepared to grow stronger. The Greek Jews had not gone back to the traditionalists. They were more flexible. They had been flexible enough to leave their old beliefs for Judaism and they retained their pliancy.

Paul and Barnabas came down through the steep dangers of the mountains, now more hazardous than ever with snow, icy streams, and hungry men. But they reached Perga safely, and from Perga went to the white seaport of Attalia where they found a ship which hugged the coast to Seleucia.

8

BACK TO ANTIOCH
Escape from the Law's Bondage

Great was the welcome home. Paul and Barnabas set before the church at Antioch "an open door which no man could shut." It was the door which God had opened "of faith to the Gentiles."

The Antiochene Christians were men and women capable of great rejoicing. They were quick to see that the journey of Paul and Barnabas had been carried out with a decisiveness which made it quite different from the loose peregrinations of wandering philosophers or the formal missions of the synagogues.

It had followed a pattern which the Christian community in Antioch already found very useful—a sort of divine dialogue which engaged the Christians and the pagans in increasingly fresh and lively ways; it drew very little from the past.

It was an exchange which had only a nominal regard for the community in Jerusalem. The Antiochenes knew, by the very heterogeneity of their own leaders, that the needs, the temperaments, the urgencies of the Greek world differed profoundly from the homogeneous problems of the community in Jerusalem.

But the Jerusalem Christians, aware of the loosening holds, deeply, primordially uneasy of the pagan world, became alarmed at Antioch's broad invitation to the Gentiles. Christians from Jerusalem came to Antioch to protest, warn, and demand that the uncircumcized must not be accepted straight out of their paganism with no commitments required of them, but must come through the door of Judaism, accepting the discipline and taking upon themselves the token of that covenant with God, circumcision.

The Antiochene leaders were startled; they temporized, but Paul flew into a rage. He and Barnabas had spent a year of hardships and dangers to bring into the fold those pagans whose souls yearned for a spiritual life free of the ritual of knives and the smell of blood. And now the circumcision knife was thrust before their eyes.

Paul's words were fierce. He called the Jerusalem Christians, "false brethren" (he thought they might even be political spies) "who came in privily to spy out our liberty which we have in Christ Jesus, that they might bring us into bondage."

Paul, having himself escaped from such a deep bondage to the rigidity of the law, saw this assault as a matter of life and death for Christianity.

His work in Tarsus and Syria, his journeys with Barnabas to Cyprus and the desolate mountains of the moon had not been work done in a corner. The success of Antioch itself was an old story. Why this monstrous inhibition now, when their labor was beginning to embrace the world?

Barnabas and the Antiochene Christians were probably as articulate in protest as Paul, for the whole principle of salvation by grace would be toppled over if the Gentiles were required to fulfill the law of Moses before they could enjoy the universal law of grace. If this were demanded, then the promise given to forlorn men and abandoned women in Pisidia, to the young shepherds in the Lycaonian plains, to the lame man in Lystra, to the spiritually underfed who had swarmed in the desolate outpost of Derbe, was without the slightest meaning. The Greek considered the Jew a barbarian for mutilating his body by circumcision. This feeling must be taken into account and the fact clearly faced that if the legalists had their way, the Gentiles might cease to respond and Christianity wither away as a Jewish "heresy."

As far as Paul was concerned there could not be a

tincture of compromise. The legalists must be resisted until every misunderstanding had been cleared away. There was a bitter irony in this, for many times he must have longed for the familiar nobility of Judaism—"the glory and the covenants and the giving of the Law"—to cut through the inchoate confusion and moral anarchy of the Gentiles. Outward signs and symbols were far easier to require than a changed heart.

But it was "Christ which had broken down this middle wall of partition," and Paul's insight told him that the whole future of Christianity hung on this spiritual issue and that it must be settled now and forever.

The Antioch church agreed. Paul, Barnabas, and "some of the others" were appointed to return with the legalists to Jerusalem where the question would be raised and answered.

Paul acted pragmatically and took a witness. He took Titus.

Titus was a Greek. He was a son of Plato, not of Abraham. In the church of Antioch he had been tried and tested. He may have been brought into the church by Paul; he was, in any event, "my true child after a common faith."

The Antiochenes went first to "those pillars," as Paul called Peter, John, and James, who welcomed them in all good fellowship. Had it been left to these three the pure empiricism of success among the Gentiles might have been sufficient. But "some believers who belonged to the party of the Pharisees" demanded that the whole issue be made a matter of communal debate. Paul as a Tarsian

Jew and Barnabas as a Cypriote Jew knew the subtly inferior position in which all members of the Diaspora were held. This may have accounted for some of the difficulties with the Jerusalem Christians, innocent reflecters of a prejudice. The attitude was barely noticed when things went well; in a crisis it delicately manipulated the thoughts of the legalists.

The issue was both a simple and a subtle one, and it went back to the days of Saul the avenger: as long as Christians lived in Judea persecutions were a continual threat and would inevitably have a political impetus. To remain devoted to the Mosaic law would remove one cause of danger, for their legal position as a sect of Judaism gave them the protection of Judaism—but this protection had no legal validity to Rome without the mark of circumcision.

Judaism also prevented the great danger of losing the Messiah as a national hope and seeing him absorbed into the Kyrios cults which existed all over the empire. Jesus, a Jew, had come to the Jews. He had said, "I am not come to destroy but to fulfill the Law." The Jerusalem Christians were devoted Jews and, for many good reasons, did not wish Jews and Christians to have any kind of wedge driven between them. To attack Jew was to attack Christian, and vice versa. A bloody massacre had taken place during the Passover in the year 48 A.D., which is usually accounted the year of this meeting. The city was filled with pilgrims, the Romans had increased their guards on Antony's Tower, "for a body of men in arms invariably mounts guard at the feasts," Josephus wrote in describing the event. One of the soldiers engaged in a lewd act in the sight of the Jews gathered below in the Temple. Crying out to the Procurator Cumanus to avenge them, some of the younger men threw stones at the soldiers. Troops poured into the Temple court and in the panic twenty thousand were killed. "The feast was turned into mourning for the whole nation and every household into lamentation" . . . Christian households as well as Jewish.

Let Jew and Christian be united by the Law the Christians urged; let us stand together. In this vicious, sensual world, circumcision represented a commitment to a life of decency and order. Christian converts were seldom drawn from officialdom or the aristocracy. They were mostly poor men and women, caught in the pain of the world—thieves, prostitutes, drunkards, or men and women who could never be sure that the security they had reached would not vanish in the helpless sweep of change. The Jerusalem Christians believed they would fail in compassion and responsibility if they sent these new Christians into the bloody arena of life armed only with an untried faith. Give all these the strong wall of the Judaic law.

It was an argument no sane man could reject unless he had an incontrovertible reason to put in its place.

Paul understood this as well as any man. Barnabas understood it, and all those who had labored under the rampant and official vices of Daphne's grove in Antioch. But these men believed that a profounder security lay in the desire to imitate the life of Jesus. Paul said, "He is not a Jew who is one outwardly, but he is a Jew who is one inwardly, and circumcision is of the heart. . . ." To him circumcision was not a means of grace; circumcision raised a confidence that could be both false and inhibiting. "In Christ Jesus, neither circumcision availeth anything, nor uncircumcision; but faith which worketh by love."

He took as adamant a position against those who made an esoteric virtue out of being uncircumcized as he did against the legalists. Circumcision must not be allowed to serve a spiritual purpose one way or the other. Faith, rich and bounteous, put the seal of the covenant on man and determined his relation to God and his service to Christ.

Paul went so far in his sharpness and anger as to fling before them a comparison to the frenzied rites of emasculation by which the priests of Cybele looked for salvation. He was heard with horror and alarm. Agree with Paul and step by step they would have to relinquish the details of the Law which had maintained the integrity and identity of the Jewish people through all the hazards of persecution and dismemberment. The Law was their political, criminal, and religious code.

In Pisidian Antioch Paul had refused to concede that a slave had to be legally free before he became a Christian or that a woman had to change her sex; now he refused to yield one degree. He was determined to protect the man reborn. The Christ of Paul did not belong to the Jews any more than he did to the Greeks or the barbarians.

He said, "We are upright by faith in Christ, not by doing what the Law commands, for all that can defile a man are the thoughts of his own heart."

The legalists demanded, "Has God made another door to himself outside the Law of Moses? Has he made us free from the law of sin?" Paul was already aware that many of the Jerusalem Christians still found it impossible to sit down at meals with Gentile Christians though Jesus had set the example, and Peter had, in a vision, received the command to call no man unclean. This refusal was a middle wall of partition as adamant and grievous as the dividing wall in the Temple beyond which no Gentile could go without risk of death.

Sustaining the position of Paul, Barnabas, and the men from Antioch was their success in Antioch, Cyprus, Galatia. Titus standing in their midst, a Greek in limbs and mind, a Christian in heart and spirit, was a testimony to the free exercise of whatever was true, honorable, just, pure, lovely, and praiseworthy in the service of the Christ.

Paul closed the door to any compromise by demanding that the community in Jerusalem either confirm the work that had been done in Galatia and Antioch or say plainly that it had been done in vain.

He gained one point after the other. At length Peter rose and supported Paul with vivid words. "God who knows the heart bore witness to the [Gentiles] giving them the holy Spirit just as he did to us, and he made no distinction between us and them, but cleansed their hearts by faith." Peter recalled to them the terrible yoke

of the Law which was beyond the power of a good Jew
to observe in all its details however hard he tried. He
called the legalistic demand "tempting God. . . . But we
believe that we shall be saved through the grace of the
Lord Jesus, just as they will."

It was a long struggle and perhaps a bitter one. The
legalists had undoubtedly gained great support in the
years since James the brother of Jesus had emerged out
of obscurity. He had held the Christian community
together after the death of James the son of Zebedee in
44 A.D., and the flight of Peter from Herod's prison.
James was a very pious Jew. He went daily to pray in
the Court of Israel, he observed all the requirements of
the law, his piety was known through the whole city.
When, on this occasion, he spoke, everyone paid attention. He said, "Brothers, listen to me. Simon has spoken
properly."

He proposed to solve the problem by a division of
labor. They in Jerusalem would work among the circumcised, the Antiochenes among the heathen from
whom circumcision would not be demanded.

Peter and John and James gave their hands to the men
from Antioch.

It appeared a great victory.

James asked only that a letter go out to the Gentile
Christians requiring them to refrain from meat offered
to idols, or killed in non-Jewish ways, and from fornication.

About fornication the Gentiles were doing their best,
but the restrictions on food, though appearing a minor

request, reduced the whole victory to an equivocation.

To the Jerusalem Christians meat sacrificed to idols and then sold to the public (as was the custom) was meat not only contaminated by idol-worship but an additional source of profit to priests and pagan temples. To the Gentile Christians, however, access to this pagan meat might be the difference between eating and starving.

Protest carried some weight. The letter was addressed only to the churches of Antioch, Syria, and Cilicia where a choice of meat could be made. The churches of Paul's own ministry in Galatia were left free to eat what was available.

Yet it remained a compromise, for James had based his requirements on the rebuilding of the tabernacle of David and the acknowledgment of ritualistic feelings and practices. His reasoning was subtle, but it indisputably established grades of Christians, one a lower degree of weaker persons, unable to bear the full demand of the Law. It planted the seed of sects.

The danger of young ardent communities being broken by hard stones had been avoided, however.

Peter arrived in Antioch some weeks later to reaffirm the blessings and heal any lingering misunderstandings. Judea was still shaken by violent disorders. A servant of Claudius Caesar had been killed by brigands on a lonely road. Cumanus the Procurator had ordered all the men from the neighboring villages to be brought to him in chains. While carrying out these orders, a soldier had taken a copy of the sacred Law, torn it in pieces and flung it into the fire. When word of this reached Jerusalem outcries rent the city and Cumanus ordered the soldier put to death. But this action did not bring peace. Disorders broke out all over the land. Disorders in Judea shook Christians everywhere.

Peter brought his own lively incarnation of the Jerusalem community to which Antioch must be linked in both woe and joy. Was it not the navel and center of the faith? Must not all be one?

Peter had the capacity for entering heartily into the life of his friends. He sat down to the love feasts with the Gentiles—pagans until yesterday—and he blessed all works of brotherhood and healing.

While he was there, eating and sharing, the blow fell.

It was sharp and splitting. Certain adherents of James came down from Jerusalem and seeing the Jewish and Gentile Christians eating together raised such a storm that the community was torn in half. Perhaps the Jerusalem Christians saw that no effort had been made to follow James' stipulations to the churches in Antioch and Syria. Perhaps, even with Jewish butchers in the city, the Christians had eaten what they chose. Perhaps the Antiochene behavior seemed not only boorish but dishonest: had they not agreed to the letter? Perhaps the whole church was charged with duplicity, though Paul was the real culprit.

In any case the storm was furious. Not only the authority implicit in Jerusalem had been challenged but good faith among brethren called to account.

Barnabas, who had withstood so much, wavered. Peter, with his own great authority, yielded. Only Paul, it seemed, would not retreat.

He was certain in his soul that there could be no compromise. Christianity must have one doctrine, one salvation by grace through the workings of a man's conscience.

Paul's position was a lonely one. It drove him outside all tradition. Peter's reversion to obedience and refusal to eat with the uncircumsized shut a gate between friends who had loved and trusted each other. Sharing a meal was an immemorial gesture of trust, equality, and friendship.

Paul withstood Peter to his face. He charged Peter with being most devious of all—poor Peter who loved to love all men. "If you, though a Jew, live like a Gentile how can you compel the Gentiles to live like Jews?" And his words ring as hot and clear now as they did on the day he spoke them. "I, through the law, died to the law that I might live to God. I have been crucified with Christ; it is no longer I that live but Christ who lives in me, and the life I now live, I live by faith. If righteousness came through the law then Christ died to no purpose."

Paul could not take a step backward in time. His thoughts must have yearned toward his children of grace in the high mountains of Galatia, blessedly safe, exposed only to the dangers of hunger, wild beasts, and clay idols.

Paul had a high temper. He was a master of invective. The Antiochenes may have seen him suddenly as a splinterer from whom they must disengage themselves in order to preserve a unity. Without unity, in this roiling world, they could be picked off, one by one.

Paul asked Barnabas to go back with him into Galatia "to see how they do." Barnabas did not deny Paul outright, but he said he would wish to take John Mark, his young kinsman, with them. In the midst of all the charges and countercharges John Mark may have appeared as a link to Jerusalem, a safeguard when they stood in the pagan world of Galatia. "But Paul thought it not good to take him with them who had forsaken them in Pamphylia. And there arose a sharp contention so that they separated from each other."

It was a break inexpressibly sad, for Barnabas had been the first to see the greatness of Paul and had thrown open all the gates he could reach so that Paul might pass free and unchecked.

Barnabas took Mark and left for Cyprus. He is not spoken of again in *Acts*. Cypriote tradition says he was stoned to death by a mob raised against him by Bar-Jesus, that magus of the Proconsul who had nursed his revenge. Legend says that John Mark took his body in secret and buried it near Salamis.

Paul asked Silas to go with him and they started north.

Silas is another of those great and quiet men who speak gently across the centuries.

He was a Hellenized Jew. His Hebrew name was also Saul, his Greek name Silas, his Roman name Silvanus. He threw in his lot with Paul. He too was a Roman citizen.

Paul's break with the work in Antioch was final. He was now entirely responsible for the direction in which he moved.

9

PHILIPPI
A Colony of Grace

Walking on the narrow torturous road above the gulf of
Iskanderun Paul and Silas could see the Mediterranean
spread out before them. It reached beyond Cyprus to
Crete and to those islands which led to the west. The
time was, in all likelihood, the spring of the year 49 A.D.

They walked because holy men in Asia walked. This
land was Paul's. Cilicia and Tarsus had been his field to
plow, during those lonely private years before Barnabas
had come to fetch him.

They listened, talked, blessed, and went on. Around the Cilician Gates no country was wilder or more beautiful. Caravans, waiting to pass through the narrow defile, moved with an expert caution, for the road to the man-made gate in the mountain was edged by deep gorges and a swollen river.

When they reached the uplands, they turned north though the caravan routes lay to the east.

At this top of the world were the summer pastures of the black-haired goats who gave prosperity to Tarsus and perhaps even to Paul's own family fortune.

It was a world of brown plains, sere land, thorn grass, trees stunted by the wind. The roads were cart tracks and the villages were made of black hair tents or mud houses.

When the road narrowed between towering peaks they moved in danger of lonely outlaws and wild animals in the forests. Where there were no roads they scrambled up friable rocks. They crossed rivers by clinging to inflated ox-bladders or to ropes stretched from shore to shore.

In this world of antique decay, where abandoned citadels of Rome matched the Greek ruins, mountaineers gave them shelter, unless they slept in caves or under ledges or in hollows of splintered rock. One can be sure Paul and Silas did not walk all these miles in silence. The people might not speak Greek, but men with revelation to impart do not wait on a language. But what message did they have for these people? The message of a Jewish laborer who had been put to death as a criminal, a story that must be addressed to the lost and enslaved of Asia to whom death by torture or hunger was a present possibility. Yet within this story lay a divine reality that was the hope of the world.

They came first to Derbe and went on to Lystra. They found that Christians had held firm. In Lystra or Derbe, Timothy joined them.

Timothy is a Greek name. Timothy's father was Greek but his mother was Jewish. The marriage of a Jewish woman to a Gentile was a great sin, but the synagogue had not thrust her out, nor had Timothy been circumcised. Paul talked in these synagogues freely, with no opposition.

Timothy was a rare bird to catch in these mountains. Half-Greek, half-Jew, bred in a barbarian world, he could be all things to all men. Paul circumcised him. Paul had just fought an intractable battle against circumcision, yet he circumcised Timothy. Once Paul had established a principle, he could then use it to maneuver on the rough seas of controversy. Timothy would meet many Jews. To the Jews let the strain of his mother be the link that drew them together. "I have become all things to all men," Paul said, "that I might by all means save some."

In this spring world, where flowers grew on the sides of the black mountains, he found that his children of grace had withstood all blandishments, had attained that quality of the newborn man who sees with new eyes, hears with new ears, thinks and loves with a new mind. The new Christians had showed great courage and restraint. These Christians must reach the worshippers of the rustic little deities which infested Phrygia—the spirits of the springs, rivers, and forests, the worshippers of the god Mên, who protected men and cattle from disease or healed them when they fell sick—these people were very hard to reach with the Christian message, for their gods were, on the whole, benign. The cult of Mên was not riotous or phallic; it was homely and quiet and would, as time went on, shake these Christians as even the Great Mother Cybele could not do.

But Paul must trust Christians to multiply Christians.

He and Silas and Timothy did not linger.

With new vast ambition, they turned their thoughts to the province of Asia and to Ephesus. Ephesus was the greatest trade and banking center along the Aegean coast, the seat of a Proconsul, the third greatest city of the empire. The road to Ephesus would take them down the Lycus and Meander valleys; it was the great central route of the empire. They would preach as they journeyed.

But Paul had a vision. The spirit said, *No; do not preach the word in Asia.*

It seemed an intolerable prohibition. Two hundred miles of fertile land with no seed sown. But he did not question it. They left the trade route and turned north, plunging again into regions where life was very cheap. Here villages were subject to earthquakes and to outlaws more desperate than the villagers. The isolated inns were notorious for their filth and thievery.

Temptation must have harried them. When they

reached "opposite Mysia," they thought to make the
best of this mysterious bargain and go north to Bithynia
where many Greek cities lay on the Black Sea. But once
more the spirit said No. Beyond Bithynia lay only trading posts where Roman soldiers kicked their heels and
tried to piece together the words of Russian traders and
slant-eyed people from the regions to the east.

Paul, caught between the two millstones of his nature,
reason and revelation, must have lived with some exhaustion. Silas, heretofore safe in his city world, and
Timothy, riding a Pegasus of new young vision, were as
thwarted as Paul.

They turned west into Mysia, perhaps at Kotiaion or
farther north at Dorylaion, and came across the highlands thick with forests where the snow would soon be
falling.

This was a trackless region of narrow valleys and
yawning gorges, of cave dwellers and rock tombs, of a
mysterious religion that had some echo of Cybele in it.
Here were lost people who spoke a private language of
their own. What message could the Christians bring
to such withered minds? Why, the message was: *though
I die yet shall I live,* the word that all mankind longed to
hear to quiet the pangs of fear.

Soon the smell of the sea was drawing them on.
Harvest time had almost come and rustic bowers to
Artemis and Demeter were waiting for the first harvest
fruits. The little goddesses wore flower garlands and
much innocence. But as Paul, Silas, and Timothy drew
nearer the sea, the moral decay of this ancient world

deepened about them. The innocent garlands disappeared from Artemis' bowers, and phallic images took their place; garments stripped from worshippers hung in the branches of her sacred trees.

At last they stood above the plains of Troy. Empty, lonely, the plains of Troy spoke of glory passing and man's great need for the immemorial.

Troas was a fever-ridden seaport, a Roman colony. The Greek section was dirty, poor, and drunken, the Roman quarter was rich. Marble piers stretched into the cobalt-blue sea, and the sails of a hundred little ships danced on the water. Many visitors came to Troas to see the plains of Troy. In Troas, guides as thick as leaves promised to show the place where Achilles' myrmidons set upon Hector, or where the wooden horse passed into the gates of the city, or where Zeus and Hera performed their conjugal rites while the desperate Trojans retreated before the Greeks. Tourists carved their names (according to Strabo) on the pine trees.

Many Macedonians came to Troas, tall men, their wide-brimmed hats seen above the crowds.

Paul, Silas, and Timothy stood on the edge of the Aegean Sea, brought thus far by spiritual intuition which had been loud as a voice. Although the water might lap at their feet, it did not occur to these men to doubt that the next step would be forward. A man, identifiable as a Macedonian, stood before Paul in a night vision and said, "Come over into Macedonia and help us."

Spiritual illuminations such as this came to the intellectual, eminently practical man, Paul, again and again through his whole life. These illuminations have been rationalized and explained and qualified in a hundred ways by pragmatists, but spiritual intuition is an intrinsic element in the nature of a spiritual man.

Whenever Paul heard or saw his answer, he moved without delay. There were no intellectual weighings, no silence fragmented by doubt. At this point in *Acts*, the narrator employs a "we." If a fourth person joined Silas, Timothy, and Paul we are not told his name, but the writer of *Acts* was, by strong tradition, Luke.

Luke was a Gentile, possibly a Greek. Paul called him a physician. Legend said he was also a painter. His devotion never wavered. At the very end he was still with Paul.

They found a ship. The captain made his sacrifices to the sea and to Aphrodite; the blue pennant in honor of Poseidon hung against the sky.

Little islands, green and purple, lay like flowers on the dark sea. They came that night to Samothrace, a most strange and mysterious island, rising four thousand feet above the Aegean. In late summer the festival of the Cabeiri filled the mountain with music and moving lights, and the initiates of these mysterious gods were endowed with power to save all in danger on the sea.

Paul was merely crossing from one Roman province to another; Greece itself was dead and gone. The vitality that came with commercial wealth and trade remained in Asia. Intellectual vigor had also been left behind in the great cities which stretched along the eastern shores as far as Egypt.

What lay before them?

In Greece the fields were abandoned, commerce exhausted; the only cities with life were the Roman cities, Philippi, Corinth, and Patrae.

Beyond Greece were vast wandering barbarian tribes swarming over the great steppes to the north, filling the mountains that reached to the Adriatic, riding over the German plains, and sweeping in Celtish barbarism through Spain, Gaul, and Britain. In the center like a consummate charioteer stood Rome, holding the reins to bring them all triumphantly to the service of empire.

What a little band they were, the Christians. They could never drive the great forces of the world to do their will.

The ship was never far from land. Birds rose from the marshy islands and gulls sat on the sail and dolphins leaped in the sea which grew smooth and violet with twilight.

In two days they came to Neapolis. It lay white and marble in the sun. Its villas gleamed on the hills behind the city where the ruins of ancient towers kept a watch above the sea. On a high promontory the little temple of Aphrodite of Neapolis wore a pediment of watching gulls.

To the north and the west the great mountains of Macedonia rose in ranges steep and black.

The road twisted nearly two thousand feet into the mountains past mines of gold and silver. The ten miles to Philippi could have been a child's journey, but the precipitous road, prickly as a goat's path, made great demands on the walker. Earthquakes had shattered the rocks, and along the road were many shrines to Dis, the god of earth tremors.

From the summit of a range the road plunged to the marshy plains where Philippi lay. Here, within man's memory, Brutus and Cassius had died and with them the Roman Republic. Soldiers of Mark Antony and Augustus, who had fought on this plain, were given land and called *coloni*.

The old city from which Alexander had moved on to the conquest of Asia rose in terraces on the hills, beautiful and decayed. Its houses were Greek, its temples small and hushed. In the mountains beyond the old city the cults of Orpheus and of Dionysus had begun, time before memory, and shared the blood-drinking, flesh-eating rites of salvation.

As the Orphic worship became more esoteric and private, Pythagorian in its awareness of a higher nature in man, the Dionysiac rites became more frenzied and carnal, the death and resurrection of the god reaffirmed by the copulation of worshippers. These mountains above Philippi were still sacred to Dioynsus and unearthly cries could be heard at certain times of the year, echoing eerily above the hard official city.

This mysterious dual life of Philippi gave it a re-markable quality. Its ghost, the most archaic of Greece,

kept a silent watch over its body which had been transformed into a Roman city at its most arrogant and
brutal.

Rome had no art of its own, no original philosophy,
no scientific discoveries. Whatever it possessed was taken
from Greece. Rome bowed to the moral and intellectual
superiority of Greece, sent her sons to Athens to acquire
some of the mystique of culture, took over the Greek
gods and gave them Roman names—yet in Italy virtually
all Greeks were enslaved and Greece itself defiled by
Roman blood games in which old gladiators died to
quench the homesick longings of the colonists.

On the Acropolis the sons and grandsons of Augustus'
soldiers governed the city in the name of the Roman
Senate. Many altars to the emperor stood in public
places so that the wise citizen could have the benefit of
conspicuous devotion. Since the emperor included in
himself the pantheon of gods no separate altars to foreign
gods were allowed within the city walls of Philippi.
Mithras, who was very strong among the Roman *coloni*, was believed to have a Cave of Initiation in the
mountain close by.

However, augurs, fortunetellers (sharply and hastily
interpreting events on the run for a penny), ventrilo-
quists carried on a brisk business in this hard, commercial,
trifling city.

Why had they come, Paul, Silas, Timothy, and Luke,
straight as birds flying? Why, once again, must the
message of hope be laid before the most intractable and

hostile of witnesses? In Philippi there was not even a synagogue to temper the first shocks of salvation. Jews had built no homes in this city.

For some days they walked in the streets, stood in the marketplace, listened to the hard, oiled chatter of people washed here from Syria, Lydia, Asia Minor for small purposes, smally pursued. Bewilderment must have filled those four who had come a great distance to proclaim a new way of life, and yet were still silent.

At length they learned that a place of Jewish prayer lay outside the city gates by the river Gangites.

Such open places of prayer had been common since the days when the Jews sat down by the river in Babylon. The running water offered purification, and in song, prayer, and sermon God's presence was affirmed. Paul, Silas, Timothy, and Luke took their place among the handful of Jews. The Jews they had come to find were all women.

It is pure conjecture to assume that this confirmed a feeling Paul had held for a long time—that women were a solid rock on which to build a church—but after Philippi many women are mentioned in his letters. As he went on through Greece and back to Ephesus and on to Rome, he greeted them as pillars who held up the churches.

Christianity gave women an implicit position, spontaneous, irrepressible. Women shared, they participated. Their positions of authority within the church were based on their own merit. Many of the Christian apostles took their wives on their travels—"the other apostles

and the brothers of the Lord and Peter"—and it is hard
to fancy that the women moved in unbroken silence.

When the woman who ruled in this place of prayer by
the river extended the invitation to strangers, Paul and
Silas told of the mercy and love of God as revealed by
Jesus, whereby, rooted and grounded in love, they could
comprehend the breadth and depth and height and
length of the divine purpose of God and man and know
the love of Christ which surpassed knowledge. Thus
might they be filled with all the fullness of God, for
unto everyone is given grace according to the measure
of the gift of Christ . . . and by that grace captivity is
led captive and gifts given to men.

There were no outcries, no hesitation. The foremost
woman in the group, a Lydian whose business was the
dyeing and selling of purple goods, a luxurious business
and a highly skilled craft, said she believed and wished
to make a sign of her commitment.

Paul seldom engaged in the ancient rite of baptism,
but, moved perhaps by this extraordinary occasion
when the words they had spoken were received with
swift delight, he baptized her.

Lydia, or the Lydian from Thyatira in the province
of Asia, persuaded them to stay in her house, and her
entire household was baptized.

To come to Macedonia to make a church of women
at the direction of a vision had a divine irregularity
about it, and this church was the one he loved the most
—it came to him whole and remained intact. It went
from grace to grace.

As they went about this city of avarice and cunning, listening with the ears of God, watching for the lambs of God, a slave girl cried after them day by day. She had the power of foretelling, she was a ventriloquist, one of those pythonesses common to the Greek cults who, drugged and half-witted, wandered the roads of the East, chained to their masters. They were debased members of the oracular profession which had reached its apogee at Delphi. In this city of brisk commercialism, where fortunetelling and potions preceded most business undertakings, she brought great prosperity to her masters.

Now she followed Paul, crying, "These men are the servants of the Most High God which show unto us the way of salvation," and her cries drew great attention to Paul. "Most High God" was what the pagans called Jehovah, but it was also the name given to Attis, Zeus, Apollo. The way of salvation was the invitation offered by all cults to the curious.

Paul, endeavoring to speak against her cries, made a poor show of himself. At length he was obliged to force an end, for nothing could be heard except her voice. He said, "I command thee in the name of Jesus Christ to come out of her." Her madness left her.

Paul had done as Jesus did. He had not laid the sin on the sinner, nor the madness on the poor bedeviled human. Identity was reclaimed.

The girl could no longer prophesy, she could no longer find even a lost pin. She was no use whatever to her owners. Their outrage was measured by their previous prosperity. If the trickery of these Jews could break one man's fortune, the whole commerce of the city was in danger.

They seized Paul and Silas and dragged them into the agora where the praetors waited daily to dispense judgment.

Casting out demons affected a crowd almost as profoundly as raising the dead. A man's whole life was spent placating demons in one way or another. Only great holy men knew the unique words by which the princes of the dark could be controlled. Paul had cast out a demon in public. There was no doubt about it. The crowd thronged and shouted, confident of the presence of mighty magicians.

The owner of the slave would be obliged to make a charge that cut through the emotion of the crowd. The charge was unruly action against Rome.

"These men, being Jews, exceedingly trouble our city and teach customs which are not lawful for us to receive, neither to observe, being Romans."

The result was all that the owner intended. The charge was in effect treason, and the crowds had no desire to be brushed by treason.

The praetors ripped at their garments in ritualistic outrage. They sentenced Paul and Silas to be beaten by the lictors who attended the magistrates on all public occasions and to be thrust into the inner prison where their feet would be chained to the wall.

It was against the law to beat Roman citizens. Perhaps Paul and Silas cried out and lost their protests in the louder cries of the throng. When they had been beaten, they were hustled to the prison and thrust into the hands of the captain of the prison who was cautioned by every adjuration known to man to hold them safe. The torches barely illumined the inner room where they were chained, and when the captain took away the torches the darkness was complete.

Their clothes stuck to their bloody backs, the stench of the prison was sickening, the blackness canceled time, but after awhile they began to sing. All around them in the blackness, in cells beneath them, were men immured from light, hopeless, buried alive. They heard the song of angels, of the underworld, of the judgment day. There was a great rending of the earth, chains were dragged from the walls, and the doors of the prison flung open.

This land of earth tremors had joined in the songs.

The captain, still heavy with sleep, prepared to take his own life presuming his prisoners had fled. But Paul called out to reassure him, and the captain sprang down the steps, carrying a torch.

The captain was a Roman. Whether he was tall, short, young, old, what springs of despair, what joy, grief, or readiness had brought him to this moment, one cannot know. But his response to Paul and Silas, there in the guttering light of the torches, was to fall on his knees and ask, "What must I do to be saved?"

Paul had one answer at all times, "Believe on the Lord Jesus Christ"—that is, be renewed in the spirit of your mind.

The Roman took them into his house, washed their wounds, gave them food, asked them to talk to his household of the new birth required of the new man.

When it was day the lictors knocked at the door. The magistrates had sent word that the Jews were to leave the city without delay. Earthquakes might be common in this land, but earthquakes following a formidable display of magic were profoundly alarming.

With some bitter humor, Paul declined to be thrust secretly out of this city where he had gained Christian friends. "The magistrates required us to be beaten and they cast us into prison. Now do they imagine they can thrust us out secretly? We are Roman citizens. Let them come and fetch us."

Paul was tired of harassment. If he could stand on indisputable rights he would be able to give dignity to the whole Christian community. The lictors were filled with dismay. The beating of Roman citizens was an offense of such gravity that their offices might be forfeit. The magistrates were equally dismayed and came themselves, saying, "We did not know the truth about you, that you are righteous men." And they implored Paul and Silas, "Depart from this city lest they again make a riot."

But Paul and Silas would not agree until they had seen their friends. They found them in the house of Lydia where they comforted and encouraged them and made some plans for the future.

Silas and Timothy went on with Paul down the mountains, along the Roman Road. Luke, it seems, remained in Philippi. They went in a new wisdom. Their torn backs reminded them of old familiar humiliation, but their minds were more wary, more agile, more resolved to be wise as serpents and harmless as doves.

Map labels: MACEDONIA, Philippi, Amphipolis, Neo-polis, Thessalonica, Samothrace, Beroea, AEGEAN SEA, Troas, AEOLIA, Pergamum, Lesbos, Eleusis, Chios, IONIA, Corinth, Athens, Ephesus

10

THESSALONICA
The Mystery of Freedom

The Roman Road to Amphipolis, a provincial capital of Macedonia, was paved with marble flags. Making and maintaining these roads had been a point of honor with the Caesars since Augustus; imperial grants were given to supplement the taxes, and the "curators" of the road were state officials.

Trees had been planted to temper the heat and frequent wells invited the traveler. To their right the bare black mountains rose range on range from the red earth; to their left was the brilliant sea.

The city of their choice was Thessalonica. Thessalonica was great and prosperous because it stood on the gulf of Salonica and was a Roman naval station. It was watered by two rivers and half circled by mountains which became red in the setting sun. In the distance lay Thessalian Olympus, snow-crowned, and the lesser peaks of Ossa and Pelion. Thessalonica was Greek in its beauty; it was a free city ruled by politarchs. But it was also heterogeneous and corrupt. Everywhere in the city stood the cold formality of emperor-worship like thin, faceless wardens warning that, in the end, all power lay with Rome.

Thessalonica had a strong community of Jews. The apostles sought out the synagogue—the largest of the Diaspora except the one in Alexandria. Greeks came to this synagogue and were forever asking questions and dreaming over the answers. Greek women of the city whose husbands held authority sat among the Jewish women.

The synagogues of Thessalonica were rich. They paid large tributes to the Temple. These synagogues (as well as those of Alexandria) had a vague reputation for political devotion and of money to the Zealots. This was, of course, most private, most intimate. Their well-being and security lay in discretion.

But a vague anti-Semitism was stirring through the empire, for the Jews were the only subject peoples who had not yielded to emperor-worship, that convenient cross-fertilization of theophany. The Romans considered emperor-worship their superb answer to religious and political dissension. The lonely indigenous proselytizing of the Jews was beginning to disturb many in authority, and they made no distinction between Christians and Jews. In Rome, only a few months before, Jews had been driven from the capital in spite of Claudius' edict of toleration, because they followed a leader named Chrestus.

Everywhere the Romans were determined to have their intractable peace, and they were beginning to find that these brilliant civilized people with their religious independence were pushing their patience to the breaking point. Judea had lately been torn again by such uprisings that a score of Jews had been crucified by the legate in Syria and eighteen others beheaded. Two of the high priests, and other Sadducees in authority, had then been sent to Rome where the young king Agrippa pleaded their case so eloquently with Claudius Caesar that Cumanus the Procurator was replaced. In Egypt disorders of such magnitude had followed a visit by certain notable Jews that the Roman authorities forbade any alien Jews to come into Egypt.

Legends about Paul must have been growing in this atmosphere of sick excitement and political despair. Jewish agents of the Zealots had, in all likelihood, watched him from Antioch to Troas, for his message of a messiah was put so cryptically that he might be offering all things to all men. Jew and Roman alike knew that a crisis was growing with a feverish speed (within this generation Jerusalem would be destroyed), and these wandering Christians with their leader Chrestus raised an inchoate hope and a sharp watchfulness.

In the synagogue at Thessalonica Paul was welcomed, his message searched for a meaning, for mysterious communications can run from place to place in most extraordinary ways when interests are dependent.

Without delay he talked of the Messiah, he called him the Lord, he called him Jesus, he said that the day of Christ was at hand. But he thrust a crucified Lord before them. He thrust the curse before their eyes because "Christ hath redeemed us from the curse of the law." This was the heart of his teaching. "Redeeming the time because the days are evil," "for though our outward man perish the inward man is renewed day by day," for "there is neither Greek nor Jew, circumcision nor uncircumcision, Barbarian, Scythian, bond nor free: but Christ is all and in all."

Here was the basis for a nation's freedom, but too many lively thoughts were raising a clamor for his spiritual message to be clearly heard. The rumor that Jesus had not died on the cross had grown with the years. If true, it canceled the curse of the cross.

Paul faced this terrible challenge with an heroic temper.

From Tarsus to Thessalonica Paul rejected an earthly king. But what he offered instead was so vivid that crowds began to gather after the first sabbath. The agitation of the orthodox mounted. Paul and Silas, good rabbis, were not barred from the Beth-hamidrash in any city of the Diaspora. During the week, men of the synagogue studied the dialectics of the Torah and rabbinic commentary. To offer to their cultivated minds a messiah who had redeemed the cross from obloquy would be to free them from all fear of Caesar's power. *Thus is the prophecy fulfilled.* . . .

But not many Jews could find this hope empiric enough for them, and anger mounted. This Messiah of salvation deprived them of their reasons for heroic action, yet did not release them from the attention of the Roman spies.

The Gentiles heard it, however, with remarkable joy, carrying the word like trumpeters "not only in Macedonia and Achaia but also every place your faith to Godward is spread abroad."

Paul loved these Gentiles with a very deep love. In this city of corruption and idolatry, where every second breath was an invocation to a familiar godling, the new seekers were willing to leave their visible reassurances—rites, idols, priests—for the invisible untried faith that demanded great character of them.

The relationships of men and women had to be stabilized. Sexual indulgence had been a requirement of their old worship; now men must learn how to take wives in holiness and honor, each remaining faithful to the other, learning a whole new way in love and not concupiscence.

They loved Paul as he knew from the love he gave to them. He did not promise them ease and comfort but a constant renewal of life. They saw this promise take shape in their lives when a new orderliness and calm prevailed. They knew it by the shared faith and brotherhood, their love and concern for each other.

For the Christian Gentile all these changes became the outward and imperative signs of an inner and absolute grace. Over and over Paul obliged them to clear the field before they planted their Christian faith. "Let the purity of your lives attest . . . let your lives in their order and sobriety testify to the renewal of your mind . . . do not transgress against your brother by dishonoring his wife."

This demand was the reverse of the injunctions laid on them by their pagan worship and so the simplest requirements had to be restated again and again. But where else could freedom be found? This was the alphabet of Christianity, and Paul and Silas endeavored to set an example which never wavered from its steady mark.

Once a week they ate a meal together, a love-feast at which all were equal.

The Stoics and the Epicureans taught the unity of man, but coldly, as a principle; love itself was absent from their concept of virtue. In the Mysteries all were equal, men and women, slaves and masters, but with no obligation to translate equality into their lives. All the savior-gods taught the renewal of life, but as a symbol not a present hope.

It was man's longing which had given form to these dreams seen in a glass darkly. All cast the shadows of profound irrepressible truth. Lust and violence cried out for love and hope.

Day by day Paul and Silas gave their admonitions. "Aspire to live quietly . . . despise none . . . love all . . . Be gentle, even as a nurse cherisheth her children. Thank God without ceasing for it is his word that works in you to joy and glory."

Thessalonica held Paul and Silas. They could not have moved on had they wished. They loved and comforted, gave courage, and showed these spiritual children how to walk.

Night and day, they set an example of prudence and diligence, as they did in every town. They worked at their trade "so that we might not burden any of you while we preached the gospel of God," "for the children ought not to lay up for the parents, but the parents for the children."

Times were bitterly hard. Rome's debasement of Greece had left farms desolate and poverty everywhere. Macedonia had barely survived a famine.

As quickly as he could Paul selected those who were strongest and most confirmed in their faith and made them overseers of this new community. Self-government carried the seal of God.

The Christians had no formal meeting places. Any welcoming roof gave hospitality. There were no rites or ceremonies. Baptism was only occasional and for some special reason. Men and women spoke as the spirit moved them. If any was in trouble all were bound to come to his aid. All lived in the bonds of freedom. At Philippi Paul had been able to build a community that held together under stress. He longed to build as strongly in Thessalonica.

When the attack began it came from many sides. The Christians were charged with cupidity and uncleanness. They were charged with beguilements; perhaps their women converts were too incredible for the licentious thought of the city.

Some of the Jews in the synagogue could not give up their desperate hope that when Paul preached the day of the Lord he was speaking the cryptic message of an earthly king. To them his message must be made clear or he would become a luxury they could not afford, for the legal security of Jews was jeopardized if any new and irregular customs were tolerated in the synagogues. City authorities must have firm means of recognizing Jews or they could not protect them. For its own protection a synagogue must move harshly against any Jew who was not a Jew.

These cynicisms and cautions joined with the inchoate fears. Haters of the Jews gave money to the odds and ends of troublemakers and whipped them into a mob. The city was brought to an uproar.

The mob, looking for Paul and Silas, attacked the house of a man named Jason. When Paul and Silas could not be found, Jason was dragged out and the cry of treason raised.

Treason was a cry that chilled the blood, for though it could be raised as easily as the cry of "Fire!" and was

much used, said Pliny, to enrich a city treasury with
fines and ransoms, it carried with it inestimable danger.
No man in authority dared be passive at such times.

Borne on the back of the great beast of a mob, Jason
and his friends were brought before the magistrates. The
charge was shouted that Paul, Silas, and Timothy "had
turned the world upside down and had now come here,"
and that Jason had received them. "They are all acting
against the decree of Caesar, saying that there is another king, Jesus."

The magistrates were shrewd and discreet. They required a security from Jason and his friends to keep the
peace, then they released them.

The magistrates thus made Jason responsible for restraining Paul.

The mildness of the judgment was of the sort to
inflame a mob.

That very night Christians took Paul, Silas, and Timothy out of the city in secret and brought them to
Beroea, fifty miles away.

Paul was deeply shaken.

The father could escape, but what about the children
left behind? Were they safe both from temptation and
bodily injury?

The children of his soul had been put under bond
by the magistrates to make sure that he did not return.
Paul believed this was a "subtlety of Satan." It was indeed an arrangement of diabolic simplicity. Had the
Christians gone against the bond, the magistrates would
probably have surrendered Jason and half the Christian

community to the full consequence of treason. Paul was helpless.

Christianity itself was scarcely twenty years old, and these Thessalonians had been Christians for only a few weeks. What faith did they have to support them? Could they know why he had left like a thief in the night? Could they endure the scorn or the prudent warnings of their old friends who wished them safe in the circle of Dionysus again?

In the map: AEGEAN SEA, Troas, AEOLIA, Pergamum, Lesbos, Chios, IONIA, Eleusis, Corinth, Athens, Ephesus, Cos, Cnidus

11

ATHENS & CORINTH
Divine Nonsense

Beroea was an old city perched on a ledge of Mount
Bermius above a marshy plain. Behind it was the barrier
of mountains which lay between Macedonia and the
Adriatic, and yet across that mountain ran the Via
Egnatia, the great highway to Rome.

It was the most populous city of Macedonia. It was the
center of emperor-worship and the home of the high
priest of the province.

The synagogue in Beroea welcomed them. During the

daily Beth-hamidrash they searched the scriptures and confirmed the word that Paul had brought.

But all his listening was directed toward Thessalonica. How did the Thessalonians resist temptation? What were they thinking? Timothy, who was young and daring, could perhaps slip back into the city unseen and strengthen them if they were faltering.

Time must be used as well and fully as possible before the rod fell again. From Pisidian Antioch to Thessalonica the word had been heard with joy, the attack had followed, the humiliation delivered, and whips, rods, or darkness driven him through the gates. There was great pain in all of this: pain in the divisions of brothers, pain that there was no time to fight the attacks when they came.

Soon troublemakers came from Thessalonica and "immediately the brethren sent away Paul to go as it were to the sea." A second charge of treason might be fatal.

Centers of the world were becoming Paul's strategy. From them Christianity could be diffused.

Though a final contest with Rome might be inevitable, the empire, with its order, power, roads, and ships must be made to serve Christianity as long as possible.

He had left Philippi for the greater city of Thessalonica, and Thessalonica for the greater city of Beroea. He would wait for God's word in the city that was the heart of Greece, in Athens.

His actions were confident. Whatever doubts and fears he may have felt were not added to the burdens of his friends. "We are ambassadors for Christ, as though God did beseech you by us . . . I know nothing by myself; he that judgeth me is the Lord."

Silas and Timothy did not go with him. Silas was to return to Philippi, Timothy to Thessalonica. If the Thessalonian interdict was lifted Timothy was to bring him word immediately.

At Mthoni Paul could find a caique going south. Sea was the natural path to Athens. Under the divine and translucent light of Greece he would come into harbor.

When Rome captured Athens, Athens was sentenced to live in a perpetual twilight, a city half-dead. The glories of her past, her temples, universities, statues, libraries, rhetoric were kept alive, but their vitality was stripped away. Rome did not wish to destroy Athens wholly, for Rome had a superstitious belief that if Greece died an element of Roman glory would die as well.

Under the brilliant light, the city gleamed with the color of its painted and gilded statues, its painted houses. The temples on the Acropolis, drenched in color, rose in pillars and altars on its sacred rock till they seemed a single great temple, dedicated first to man and then to all his gods.

Paul came to Athens, probably in August of the year 51 A.D. Here is the man, Paul, alone for the first time since he left Tarsus. In all his mind and heart he is waiting. He has been repeatedly humiliated but he cannot afford the luxury of remembering it. He is also a man who is quite at home in such a world as this, for he is no little fellow awed by the mighty forces of past and present.

In this city, wholly given to the exploitation of men's spiritual and mental needs, the synagogue seems oddly impassive. It neither responded to his message nor rejected it.

Paul walked under the brilliant sky observing how truth in its many guises was made superficial. He saw the altars to all gods, and to unknown gods so that no inadvertance might deprive a man of a pinch of good fortune.

Athenians lived in the open. Every religious cult in the world found some exponent in Athens. Any philosopher could put down his stool and claim a disciple. This was not hospitality to truth but an automatic eclecticism as though Athenians had resolved long ago to appear as eternal dialecticians. Their pride was monumental and deceived no one but themselves.

Religion had so far degenerated into the phallic cults that rhetoric or rationalist philosophy were needed to give some disguise to naked desire. This was the greatest day for the quasi-philosophers since Augustus. But nobility had passed away. Epicureans had degenerated into lovers of wine and women, Cynics had descended into peculations, and Stoics had made an apathetic value of indifference and expediency.

To maintain a degree of intellectual honor, the council of the Areopagus required a sample of the thinking and presentation of all public philosophers.

In the market place the professional philosophers,

Epicureans, Stoics, Sophists, Sceptics, Peripatetics, maintained a jealous watch but did it so deftly that they could carry on their public debating and still mark down an interloper for their reputations depended on the ability to confound and demolish all rivals. They could not afford to be surprised or to concede any new knowledge.

Paul talked to the man standing next to him in the market place. When he saw that a third and a fourth man were listening, he lifted his voice although he had to compete with a dozen professional harangers for the attention of two or three pairs of ears.

"Who is this ignorant plagiarist?" the professional philosophers demanded. "Who is this vulgar fellow of low habits who picks up anything in the street? This little man of little mind?"

Two or three who had listened more closely said he was talking of new gods, Jesus and Resurrection. New gods were a crime. Paul's skill as a speaker was his enemy on this occasion. Only the council of the Areopagus could cut him down or put some control on what he said. He was hustled off to the Areopagus.

The speech credited to Paul on this occasion may be his or may be what Luke felt he must have said. In either case it reflects the man who with uncanny discernment spoke to his hearers in the language of their comprehension. For the Jews of Antioch he had traced the prophetic line of the Messiah; for the pagans of Lystra, ignorant and superstitious, he had made nature an expression of God; for the Athenians he offered a tactful, correct, yet courageous exposition of Graeco-Jewish thought.

It was also a clever speech in which he summarized the basic tenets of the Stoics and Epicureans and daringly translated them into a Christian exposition, deeper and more valid.

The council of the Areopagus listened until he spoke of "raising from the dead," then they laughed at him. The sophisticated Athenian knew all the Asian cults loved by women. These cults had been raising the dead since the days before Xenophon.

The council promised him nothing. Without their authorization he could not speak in the market place.

This indifference of Athens served to point out his course to him. It was a lonely direction but he took it without regret. The quick, shallow, philosophic life of Athens had long ago ceased to have any meaning for hungry, tired and sick men. Paul belonged with them— the hungry and desolate.

By the end of August, Athens would be filled with strangers gathering for the Mysteries at Eleusis, the festival in honor of Demeter, Côre, Dionysus, and Triptolemus, so ancient and so honored that no one could tell its beginnings.

Paul turned toward Corinth down the road past Eleusis. August and September were the hottest months in Greece and the brilliant sky was like a brazen shield. Men said the Greek light resembled no other light in the world. It was the divine radiance of Apollo, the god whom the Greeks had given the world.

During the weeks of early August many pilgrims made sacred journeys to Eleusis, although the great procession from Athens did not take place till the nineteenth of the month. The clear, crisp, effervescent air, the flowers, the scent of pine and eucalyptus, the faces washed in joy made it a journey rich in life.

The language of the Eleusinian Mysteries fell on Paul's ears like little bells—"sweet hopes regarding the end of life and for all eternity." At Eleusis the corn died in the ground to sprout anew; to the Christian the seed and the sprout and the fruit were the same, the seed and the sprout and the fruit eternally. Exalted Greek thought moved through Christianity like a fine mist. In its purity it was an aspect of that spiritual groping in the soul of man which had shifted, reshaped itself, appeared in the worship of the savior-gods, in the symbolic experience of the Mysteries, in the incomparable statement of the Logos—all aspects of truth, one might say, appearing in constantly purer form and using an increasingly comprehensible language. When Greek inspiration was blended with Hebrew revelation a new vocabulary of salvation would be shaped.

This road of burning dust under an incredibly blue sky ran beside the honey-colored mountains above the sea, and as the pilgrims approached the walls of the precincts they lighted their torches and went onward singing.

Paul took all this to the glory of God and went on.

Corinth was reached at twilight. The city lay in a plain its only trees gray and withered olives. A half circle of mountains rose into the blue and purple dusk. Acrocorinth was a jagged rectangle rising two thousand feet from the plain. People said it was the color of a lion's skin. The temple of Aphrodite stood on its height, the greatest temple to Aphrodite in the world where a thousand sacred prostitutes drew pilgrims from the east and west.

Modern Corinth was a new, brash, and vulgar city, scarcely a hundred years old. It was dedicated to the making of money and to pleasure.

Two hundred years before, the Romans had razed the city of Tyrants and of Diogenes and had sold the Corinthians into slavery. For a hundred years only the wild goats and the gulls had lived there. Then Julius Caesar had refounded the city with Italian freedmen and homeless Greeks.

It became the seat of a Proconsul. Its temples, theatres, arenas, covered colonnades, and public baths became bywords for vice. In cities like Antioch and Ephesus, where virtue had small reward, people spoke of Corinth as the epitome of evil. Its economic life was richly sustained by the temple and by the city's position on an isthmus from which trade flowed east to Egypt, Asia, and Palestine, and west to Italy, Spain, and Britain. Generations of Greeks and Romans had dreamed of a canal across the isthmus to link east and west, but the Corinthians made a virtue of necessity and charged high rates to haul ships and goods across the narrow neck on greased sleds of wood.

Corinth had no Greek pride. Intellectual life was barely mentioned. But on the road from Athens, Paul had relinquished forever the enticing words of man's wisdom. He was determined to know nothing about the Corinthians save the demonstration of the spirit and of power.

Faith must now stand free of the wisdom of men, rooted and grounded in the power of God. Whatever pleasure he had taken in his intellectual attainments had been roughly used by perfunctory rhetoricians.

He entered Corinth in "weakness and fear and much trembling," for failure assails a man when he is alone and his spirit is flagging.

The synagogue seemed cut off from the city. This was scarcely remarkable considering the nature of Corinth.

Not many Greeks joined with the Jews in Corinth. The rawness of this city, its preoccupation with money, the blood games in the arena, and the vast commerce in vice required the Jews to separate themselves.

He who had been called to the Gentiles was obliged to search for them in the cloaca of Corinth.

They were, on the whole, the dregs of a seaport town.

From Tarsus through Galatia to the plains of Troy Paul had smashed little idols as Moses had done in the generations before him, but in Corinth the idolatry was more vicious. He was obliged to attack it from every angle, for the worship of Aphrodite permeated the city. Naked prostitutes stood in the street when twilight came, and panderers extolled their charms and skills, and children sold aphrodisiacs of the goddess. Every sailor who entered the harbor paid his homage to "armed Aphrodite" who ruled from the summit.

The nervous, excitable people of Corinth kept shrines and altars in every jut and cranny of the city. Artemis of Ephesus had her temple and cult. A great bronze statue of Athena stood in the center of the city and a temple to Apollo rose near the agora. Zeus was worshipped in his many guises as god of heaven and hell. On the crag of the Acrocorinth was a temple to Necessity and to that youngest of the pantheon, the goddess Fortune.

Though the search for pleasure—and for reassurance —made great demands on the Gentiles, many showed their hunger for more spiritual fare. From Egypt sailors had brought the worship of Isis, that mother with a child at her heart, older than Aphrodite. She was a tender mother called the Queen of Heaven, Mother of God. Her worship had spread as far as the Danube, the Rhine, the Seine, the Thames, because she set no barrier of class or race, and required the equality of women. She answered the deepest yearnings. Isis and Cybele– Demeter were two incarnations of care and love; but Isis showed a tenderness which absolved a man or woman from the need of carnal excess. In the death and resurrection of her brother-husband Osiris appeared the unquenchable demand of the soul for life without end. Isis understood all things: the broken heart, the joy, the pain, the helplessness of women and of men. In these yearnings, demands, and expectations could the Christian seed be planted.

Many strange fish began to swim into Paul's net.

"Not many wise men after the flesh, not many mighty, not many noble are called. But God hath chosen the foolish things of the world to confound the wise, and God hath chosen the weak things of the world to confound the things which are mighty, and base things and things which are despised to bring to nought things that are."

It is certain that Paul listened to the weak and foolish with great love and no surprise. He called them affectionate names: fellow-workmen, fellow-slaves. Many were sullen, beaten by the viciousness of their lives. They had no further depth into which to sink. If one chose to call them rabble he would be speaking in kindness.

Paul had to lead them first into some form of moral order, some respect for their bodies, before he could address their spirits.

These broken reeds and lame dogs must be counted on to heal the sick, raise the dead, freely receive, freely give, do greater works than Jesus. One must doubt one's sanity and magnify one's faith to confront this fact.

But first they must be confirmed in their true identity, lifted out of fear, set down in honor, men and women newborn.

The genius of Paul lay in his ability to be all things to all men. He moved by an ordered faith, not knowing where it would take him. He had come to Corinth looking backward: physically tired, mentally discouraged, spiritually waiting for the words his heart longed for: Come back to Thessalonica.

This is why his life in Corinth is so intensely moving, so vibrant with the perpetual aspect of surprise. God had led him to Corinth so subtly, so simply, so incontrovertibly (when the means were all measured), that when his waifs and strays of Corinth were cleaned and decent they became the cherubim and seraphim of a naïve miracle, energetically filling the air with joyful noise and busily demonstrating the nonsense of careful plans when a divine event was waiting.

Nothing human was foreign to Paul.

He spoke in the synagogue, he tended Beth-hamidrash, he found work and friends, he went into the alleys, the pothouses, the market place, to look for the lost and forsaken.

The synagogue heard prophetic scriptures enlarged. Some heard it with great joy, some heard only the stumbling block of the cross.

Work at his trade went hand in hand with his uncanny gift for friendship. An Asian Jew named Aquila had a business of leather goods, tent- and sail-making; he had a Roman wife named Priscilla. They were, in all likelihood, Christians for they had been driven from Rome when Claudius acted against those Jews who were adherents of the Jewish agitator, Chrestus. Aquila took Paul into his shop and his home. A threefold affection of work and fellowship followed.

As for the shocking odds and ends of humanity who

drifted into his net, thieves, drunkards, boy-favorites, prostitutes, slaves, he taught them to believe in miracles: that they were not alone, that they were not abused and helpless, that the rich were not greater than the poor or men received into the kingdom of heaven before women, that the Fatherhood of God and the brotherhood of man were the archstones of the life in Christ.

Certain wealthy Greeks came to him and they were also welcomed.

Potters, shopkeepers, bronze workers, dockers filled the gap between the very rich and the very poor.

When Silas and Timothy at length arrived with word from Thessalonica and Philippi, Paul had ceased to look backward. The world of Corinth had captured him.

Silas and Timothy brought word good and bad. For all he knew—and Paul knew so much of human behavior —this would always be the case. Probably in Galatia and Cilicia at this moment good news and bad hovered like hawks over the dovecotes. He could not be all places at once.

Timothy and Silas told him the good news first. Philippi was like a rock. In Thessalonica all his true friends loved him. The heart of the community held firm in spite of provocation, in spite of the fact that everything must be tested as though it were the first day of creation. But enemies surrounded them. They told the Christian Thessalonians that Paul had abandoned them, told others that his appeal had been a deceit, that he had flattered them for his own self-aggrandizement and then surrendered them to persecution and suffering.

Though Silas and Timothy were there to refute this, the charges had shaken some converts who became slothful, quarrelsome, and sullen. A Christian way of life was so new that it was easy to slip back into the old paganism.

Paul, Silas, and Timothy knew there were no precedents, that each step must be taken for the first time. If rituals were to be abandoned, what must be put in their place? Constant love, attention, the sound of a voice?

Who first proposed a letter to the Thessalonians is not known. The proposal was an inspiration, for Paul had the extraordinary gift of putting his thoughts into vivid words. He knew the miracle of simple and compelling language. The letter that went to the Thessalonians was not formal. It was designed to be read aloud and to reproduce the sound of his voice. It was an extraordinary letter. The tone was absolutely true.

"We give thanks to God always for you . . . remembering without ceasing your work of faith, and labor of love, and patience of hope in our Lord Jesus Christ, knowing, brethren, beloved, that God has chosen you. For our good news came to you with power and spirit and ample conviction on your part. Never did we use flattering words, as you know, or a cloak of covetousness. Nor of men did we seek glory, neither of you nor yet of others. And you recollect how we worked at our trade day and night so as not to be a burden to any of you. . . . You have became an example to all the believers in Macedonia . . . for they themselves report what a welcome we had among you and how you turned from idols, to serve a true God."

He praised them for the love they showed one another. He did not suggest that the way would be easy, but by the testing of their faith would their lives and expectations blossom.

To those who had lost heart, who had grown sullen and difficult, he spoke candidly. He said responsibilities could not be evaded, and that in the end the wayward might have to find their course through disappointment.

He knew that men could find great hope and joy in this mental freedom and forget that their outer lives must be disciplined. Sexual responsibility was essential. Brotherly trust and love was imperative. A Christian life spoke more than a thousand words.

His gratitude, his love for them, infused the letter. "May the Lord make you increase and abound in love to one another and to all men, as we do to you."

There were still hints of political expectations—"that the day of the Lord had come"—and he promised he would write another letter taking these things into account. Meanwhile his tenderness reached out to them. "Support the weak, be patient toward all men. See that none render evil for evil, but ever follow that which is good among yourselves and to all men. Prove all things. Hold fast that which is good. In everything give thanks. And the very God of peace sanctify you wholly, for you are the children of light and the children of the day, you are not of night nor of darkness. Greet all the brothers and sisters with a holy kiss. I charge you that

this letter be read aloud to all of you. The grace of our
Lord Jesus be with you."

A great man's greatness closed every gulf of difference
between him and the wide diversity of humankind. He
knew all fears and temptations and triumphs; he knew
also the ineffable relations of God and man, the well beloved.

It was probably Timothy who returned to Thessalonica with the letter.

The legend of Paul had coiled its way to Corinth.
He was a stone which had agitated too many quiet pools
for him to expect peace in Corinth. He knew all that was
said: that he was the man who carried the secret message
of the King coming in his glory, that he was the divisive
agent of Rome, that he was the spokesman for a great
prophetic promise.

The synagogue suddenly split in two because of Paul.
To preach that a man hanged from a cross was the
redeemer was to blaspheme against the word of God;
to call a spiritual leader the Messiah was to defraud them
of a redeemed homeland for a united people under a
Davidic king.

Conscientious men cried anathema. Here in Corinth Paul probably received further ritualistic blows
—"forty minus one." He, in turn, shook out his garments against them. "Your blood be upon your own
heads. I am innocent. From now on I will go to the
Gentiles."

Many Jews in the synagogue went with Paul. The chief of the synagogue, Crispus, asked for baptism.

Those who left the synagogue were made welcome in the home of Titus Justus next to the synagogue.

Jesus, the disciples, Paul, all stressed the empiric acts of brotherhood. In Corinth the act of sitting down at table on the first day of the week and breaking bread together was a device so simple, brilliant, and explosive that it set forth the full term of the brotherhood of man. It was the Lord's Supper in the light of true discipleship.

In the worship of Dionysus, Serapis, Orpheus, meals were eaten together, but not quietly, in affectionate fellowship. The gods' meals were accompanied by hysteria, ecstasy, and drunkenness. But this Christian riffraff, these rich and poor, masters and slaves, men and women, sat down in love together, equal in the sight of God and each other. They sang a psalm, they pledged anew that none would be used for any wicked end, or commit fraud, or theft or adultery, or break a solemn word, or deny a trust, or honor any but the one God and father. Then they waited on each other, eating from the same dish, drinking from the same cup—overturning, the world's way.

Afterwards anyone could speak as the spirit led him —though Paul was too wise to let an ecstatic garbling of tongues pass for inspiration. "God is not a God of confusion but of peace . . . let all things be done decently and in order." And, perhaps ironically, he suggested an interpreter if more than one tongue was being used. "I would rather speak five words with understanding than ten thousand in an unknown tongue."

Each must be considerate of others in the length of his speech.

Be courteous. Comfort one another. Learn from one another. Love one another, for love builds up. Let there be a standard of teaching and a pattern of sound words. Share with those in need. Let fellowship be not in words only but acts. Pray without ceasing—let your life attest your words.

Let women's heads be covered.

Here the social revolution of Christianity came in five words.

By law, an unmarried woman, without the protection of father, brother, husband, or widowhood, was obliged to leave her head uncovered. She was helpless and vulnerable. She had no position. But to wear a veil on her head was to acquire power, honor, and dignity. With the veil she could go anywhere with security and respect.

Greek and Roman women had been somewhat emancipated from the veil, but Paul was concerned that not the lowest be forgotten. Even prostitutes who wore their long hair flowing were included in his compassion. "If a woman have long hair it is a glory to her."

It is hard to believe that Paul restricted women in the church. He was too clear and exact about equality to equivocate with a principle. He sent greetings repeatedly to women in the communities and some of them were elders. He was of course a great stabilizer. His counsel that husbands and wives not leave each other without good cause, or slaves leave their masters abruptly, was in the wide effort to build stable foundations. He knew that the outer experience must bear testimony to the inner, that freedom must come from within.

Corinth was the most Gentile of his churches. The Corinthian church was also the one which caused him the greatest despair. How in fact *does* a man destroy idols which are so easy to worship, so hard to relinquish? How *does* a man's faith survive when he goes from trouble to trouble seeing the endless folly and vexation of human behavior? How *does* he keep his patience, keep his love, keep his wisdom, refuse to yield to the exigency of the moment? In a night vision God said to Paul, "Be not afraid, but speak and do not be silent; for I am with you and no man shall attack you to harm you; for I have many people in this city."

So he stayed a year and six months, teaching life in Christ, patiently laying stone upon stone.

The vitality of this church gushed out like a spring. The word went out to the whole of the province. He taught, instructed, loved, cherished in this Greek city under the burning sky with the great tawny mountains behind.

In Corinth he was able for the first time to judge his work, to become conscious of its character, to make lucid and precise his presentation, to count all the means of attaining his end, to see the points of danger.

The dangers were many: the sharp social cleavage within the church; the cults from which so many had emerged but which continued to beckon and tempt, rationalize and confuse; the unsteadiness of those who had left the old ways and yet surrendered easily to hysteria and ecstasy in order to cover up their yawning fears.

All reliance on overt signs must be stripped away from the idol-worshippers—and from the Jews, as well, who held to circumcision. An impeccable purity of doctrine must distinguish this church in a city of blind corruption.

He was determined not to be driven away until he had done his work.

He knew that the anathema pronounced by his enemies continued to burn like a fever. He was their blight and their burden.

When the great basilica of Corinth was occupied by a new Proconsul, Lucius Junius Gallio, the brother of Seneca, the synagogue determined to bring a charge against Paul. Paul was thrust before Gallio as Gallio sat on the judgment seat.

"This fellow persuades men to worship God contrary to law."

It was a serious charge with a subtle use of the word "law."

But Gallio was a Stoic philosopher, a man with a reputation for gentleness and balance of character, and he saw through the maneuver with extraordinary ease. He chose to give the word law a Jewish sense, not a Roman. He said, "If it were a matter of wrongdoing or crime I should have reason to pass judgment. But this is a matter of words and names and your own law. See to it your- selves. I refuse to be judge of such things."

His lictors drove Paul and his accusers away.

Paul recognized what Gallio had done. He had stated an imperial policy of freedom of speech, and Paul saw how it could be used to lead him to Rome—not necesarily to the city of Caesars, but to the Roman world of Greek and Jew, Persian, Egyptian, Scythian, bond and free, where all could be made one in Christ.

The Corinthians had tried him to the breaking point, but out of it had come his richest experience in Christian power. The fruits were noble—deformed characters made straight, deformed limbs made sound.

He lingered a while longer, and when Aquila resolved to go to Ephesus where luxurious tents were a favored commodity, Paul made his move also.

The word had spread across Macedonia to Adriatic cities. It had spread through Achaia. This meant that the net had been flung over Greece.

Paul had a remarkable sense of cohesiveness. Though he had demanded his right to work with the Gentiles, he saw the work as a whole. He knew that the threefold cord of Jerusalem, Antioch, and the Gentile mission was needed to draw the net tight.

In March, when the seas were officially opened again for navigation, he, Aquila, and Priscilla sailed from the eastern harbor to cross the Aegean back to Asia. All this marble-white and painted world of Greece, the great

Parthenon, the Shining Cliffs of Delphi, the black and
sulphur mountains where the dying gods had lived, all
these templed and flowered islands which lay on the sea,
took no notice of their going, but it was the Christians
would rule here in the end.

12

EPHESUS &
JERUSALEM AGAIN
One Message in Multiplicity

Paul knew the power of Ephesus; it could scatter the word.

Its commercial power was challenged only by Tarsus. It was one of the greatest banking centers of the world because the temple of Artemis (one of the seven wonders of the world) was so inviolate that foreign kings and merchants deposited money in its vaults for safekeeping. The temple lent money, secured by mortgages, throughout the East. The basis of the city's solvency was the awe in which the goddess was held. The belief in her power brought traders in gold, silver, pearls, fine linen, wheat, beasts, and chariots from China, India, Persia, Rome. Traders, in turn, built a great commercial city, and a great commercial city provided an awesome climate in which a goddess could rule. Diligent ecclesiastical authorities wove commerce and awe together in the festival of Artemis which drew pilgrims from all over the world during the months of March and April.

Artemis of Ephesus did not have the erotic splendor of Aphrodite of Corinth but she was a great favorite of kings and rich men. The one hundred and twenty-seven pillars of her temple (jasper set in Pirian marble) had each been given by a king; gold, not mortar, was reputed to seal the joints between the blocks of marble, and her statues were of pure silver, the gifts of merchant princes.

Looked at from the sea—at high noon or sunset or by the first light of day—the reds and blues and gold of the temple were so animated that the temple seemed to wheel and radiate within a system of its own. Yet this Artemis had little relation to the chaste sister of Apollo. This Artemis was a very ancient moon-goddess whom the Greek colonists at Ephesus, eight hundred years before, had found ruling over the marshes. And all the magnificence of the temple could not obscure the fact that the object of the present sophisticated traffic in worship was a shapeless black meteoric mass hidden in a small room of the temple.

Paul prepared to go to Jerusalem for the Passover, and then he would return to Ephesus. Before he left he spoke

in the synagogue, because he always affirmed his Jewish-
ness and because the synagogue was the legal protector
of the Christians. "When they desired him to tarry
longer, he bade them farewell, saying, I must by all
means keep the feast in Jerusalem but I will return again
if God will."

He left the tending of any first fruits to Priscilla and
Aquila.

The journey to Caesarea was dangerous at this early
season. Captains sacrificed morning and evening to
Poseidon, their only mariner. Spring tempests came up
without warning. Seamen had no compass; reefs and
shoals were unmarked. Paul speaks of being shipwrecked
three times. Between Ephesus and the headland of Lycia
lay the hulks of many dead ships. When they came into
the open sea on the run past Cyprus to Caesarea the
sailors had only the stars by which to steer, and only
their oblations and prayers to carry them through the
cloudy nights.

He went alone, although by now he had many friends,
men with Greek and Hebrew names—Tychicus, Sopater,
Fortunatus, Gaius, Stephanos—names, wonderfully
alive, of younger men eager to do his bidding. The
cities were knit together by their going and coming, or
by their remaining, as Luke and Silas had remained at
Philippi, and Timothy at Thessalonica, and Titus in
Dalmatia.

In Jerusalem the Passover united Paul and the apostolic
community in old bonds of love and all the new wonders
of Christianity. The apostles had been almost as peri-

patetic as Paul, if tradition is believed—Thomas venturing as far as India, John Mark to Libya, Peter to Cappadocia, Bithynia, Libya, Greece, and Rome (Jerome, writing in the fourth century says Peter came to Rome first in 42 A.D.), John to cities in Asia where Paul had not come: Smyrna, Pergamum, Sardis.

See them—these brisk, lucid men (and women too, for all we know), journeymen workers, going on foot through this teeming ancient world dense with anxiety, change, and Roman domination of sea, land, thoughts, actions, customs, and education. How could they—one here, one there—topple the power of Rome made unassailable by Roman genius?

Yet they knew that this world must be toppled.

One wonders if a Roman customs officer in some cosmopolitan seaport felt an inexplicable chill when a homespun itinerant paid his tax and went on.

In Antioch Paul learned that circumcision was again being demanded in Galatia. He was angry at the legalists for their bad faith, he was angry at the Galatians for being a stumbling foolish people who had not learned to withstand opponents from without and within. He was roused as he had seldom been roused. He wrote the Galatians a letter, beating the dust off their clothes and making them stand up like men. Then he himself came to Galatia.

Paul had returned twice to this remote world off the trade routes. Because his relation with the Galatians had been in the youth of his own experience and therefore doubly dear? Or because they needed him so badly? The synagogues were country-simple except in Pisidian Antioch where the Jewish community had all the experience of the Diaspora. The Gentile Galatians, pantheists, had a more uncomplicated identification with supernatural forces than the rest of the Greek world where the gods had become sophisticated power-figures identified with the emperors.

In the end, however, the Galatian churches disappeared. It is perhaps a futile exercise to weigh the relative merits of innocent superstition and educated sophistry.

Christian communities, woven into a strong network, seemed even more urgent now. The dangers of isolation for untried people was a constant danger. Jerusalem was a symbol of unification. Jerusalem Christians, on the other hand, were suffering greatly from the mounting political turmoil, the hardships which came from poor Judean harvests and disjointed trade, and needed the support of all the sister churches.

Years before, Paul had taken assistance to the Jerusalem community; now he planned to raise money again, among the Galatian and Asian and Greek Christians in order to make them aware of their responsibilities to each other. In this way two blessings would be assured. Presently he would send Timothy or Titus into Galatia, Tychicus and Trophimus into Asia, Sopater and Aristarchus into Greece to gather the money.

He took the road which led him past Pisidian Antioch down through the highlands to Ephesus. He came to Ephesus with the fall rains.

Pergamum was the capital of Asia but Ephesus was

the city of the Proconsul. Its constitution was Greek, it was ruled, in effect, by the demos; an assembly met three times a month presided over by an executive known as the town clerk.

But real power of an even more potent form lay with the Asiarch, who was custodian of the emperor-cult, and with his predecessors. Each Asiarch, elected for four years, was known as the High Priest of Asia. His sole ostensible duty was to provide out of his own funds the annual festival in honor of the emperor, but since the cults of emperor and Artemis provided the greatest revenue for the city, the Asiarchs became servants of the enormous investments in cultish worship.

Ephesus lacked the sharp and superficial brilliance of Corinth; the claim it laid upon mens minds emanated from that turgid and dark region where all gross superstitions abound. Asia, with a long experience of despair, had brought forth many supernatural antidotes, many superstitions. Every form of necromancy was practised in Ephesus, and whatever integrity the ancient religions and culture possessed had been lost in the dark maze of commercialized credulity.

Paul found a handful of quasi-Christians, a dozen exotic birds who had flown out of the nest of John the Baptist. They believed in Jesus as the Christ because John had proclaimed him so. Their credulity was innocent; to them the rite of baptism in itself was enough. Paul opened their eyes to the "baptism of repentance" whereby a man surrendered his old ways of thinking and put on "the mind of Christ."

Priscilla and Aquila had also found a remarkable, not to say dazzling, evidence of this Johannine proselytizing in an Egyptian Jew named Apollos. Apollos, influenced by Philo and trained in the opulent schools of rhetoric and philosophy for which Alexandria was famous, had been preaching a gnostic interpretation of scripture in the synagogues, allegoric and elusive, concluding with John's proclamation of the Saviour.

Priscilla and Aquila had taken him briskly in hand and explained the nature of the Christ. The character of these three is disarming: Apollos with his intellectual brilliance willing to be instructed, Priscilla and Aquila able to instruct in words he could accept. When Apollos wished to go on into Greece, they gave him letters to the Christians in Corinth.

For three months Paul confined his teachings to the synagogue. His opponents were disputive but not violent. Disputations, however, took up too much time and heart. Paul was no longer in life to dispute; he wished to build. So he cut a clean swath, rented the hall of a rhetor Tyrannus and taught there daily from eleven in the morning until four in the afternoon.

This is a formidable use of time. A workman's day began at dawn, was abandoned during the hot hours of midday when he slept or played games or went to the theatre, and was resumed in the late afternoon. But from dawn to dark, Paul gave himself no rest.

The core and center of his life was—where? Teaching in a lecture room, answering questions in the tent-making shed, listening with courteous and lively eyes to a fool

or a wise man on the street, expounding, enlarging, en-
compassing, dealing with the philosophic and religious
garrulity of excited people? Himself mercurial, driven,
exasperated, he had nevertheless an unfailingly tender
voice for the individual. At such times he brought all
his blazing skill to work, all his love, all his perception.

He wished to encircle Ephesus with a ring of Chris-
tianity. Young men were sent to the cities nearby,
Colossae, Laodicea, Hieropolis, up the valleys of the
Meander and the Lycus rivers to spread this word.

Invariably they found some seeds already planted.
For twenty years Christianity had been spreading rapidly
in all directions. It had not yet become an orthodoxy so
no such thing as a Christian heresy could exist, but great
individualism certainly blossomed and strange fruits were
picked.

In the desolate volcanic land around Laodicea and Colossae beliefs in devils and pantheism were nourished and
these assumed new shapes under Christianity. Angels and
elemental spirits of the cosmos were worshipped. They
were seen in self-induced trances and these trances were
called Christian vision. The Laodicean Christians put a
great reliance on initiation within an inner sanctuary
as a means to induce higher spirituality. This amalgam
of astral philosophy, Jewish occultism, hylozoism, and
Persian mysticism plagued Paul for a long time.

One suspects that Paul's response to situations was by
now trained and trustworthy. He dealt with the world,
he was unsurprised by the world. He was able to measure,
as no ascetic could, the claims and pretensions of the

world when faced by the total simplicity of the Christ. Yet he was never far from exhaustion.

The superstitious Ephesians pursued him like peddlers. They wished both to sell and to buy. Luke says, "God wrought special miracles by the hands of Paul." To the lovers of magic, these miracles must have seemed the very acme of magic which, with a little bit of luck, they could make their own. They harried him. They tore away bits of his clothes, they claimed that evil spirits left at his touch. Ephesian charlatanism had a rawness and nastiness absent from the magic games of Cyprus and Philippi.

In this world, where there were more slaves than free men, exorcism was like a thin shrill defiance against the unappealable power of the mighty. Unless a man had some hope of exorcising his fate, he might go mad moving from one prison cell of life to another. If he were able to cast out demons he might become a little greater than Caesar.

Hysteria played perpetually on the battered minds of such men who lived on the everlasting verge of helplessness. Each was at the mercy of the man who stood above him and the gods who stood above them, and the emperor who crushed them all, gods and people. In Athens Jesus and Resurrection had been a powerful incantation. In Ephesus Jesus and Paul became the invocation.

An Ephesian named Sceva called himself a Jewish high priest (though there is no record of the name of Sceva among the high priests). He had seven sons who leaped, cavorted, used cabalistic words and symbols, and now added the name of Jesus to their incantations.

The sons of Sceva belonged to the group of magi who were teachers of a corrupt Zoroasterism—hypnotists, occultists, astrologers, exorcists with a smattering of Pythagorianism—all in all, immensely able practitioners of deceit. They pranced around a sick man, chanting, "In the name of Jesus whom Paul preaches, come out, come out!" But the sick man turned on his tormenters, beat them, tore their clothes and drove them into the street.

Paul must have thought somewhat wryly that the ways of salvation were more mysterious than an honest man could foresee. At the discomfiture of the seven sons, "Fear fell upon everyone and the name of the Lord Jesus was extolled." The downfall of the exorcists reverberated in the conscience of many of Paul's own flock who brought the amulet and secret charms, the books of magic art which they had concealed against a cloudy day, and burned them in the sight of the city. This splendid bonfire must have been watched with narrowed eyes by priests and officials, for the magic books of Ephesus were famous through the world and nourished the reputation of the city.

Paul knew that regeneration and Christian healing had to be absolutely pure and incandescent in order to be lifted above all taint of necromancy. He knew that "A great door and effectual" was opened unto him but he also knew he had "many adversaries."

He fought his adversaries for three years. In the synagogue his enemies were cold and waiting. In the streets they behaved like wild beasts. In the basilica above the prison house where the Proconsul ruled they were hard and watchful. In the temple and all the shops dependent on the temple they were artful and ingenious. But all were his enemies.

When the Great Artemis, an oak image of a female deity with a dozen breasts, was dragged through the streets of Ephesus, swaying like an old tree, on her heavy creaking cart, archaic power seemed as incontestable as wind and rain. Cast storms out of the skies forever and then attempt to cast down Artemis of the Ephesians!

Tradition (often quite as reliable as records, merely lacking their tangibility) makes Ephesus the city where Paul's imprisonments began.

Imprisonments were matters of rote. Perhaps Paul was imprisoned for not securing official authorization for his teachings. Or perhaps he was imprisoned for declining to accept the official stipend which came with the authorization of a new cult. Perhaps he was imprisoned for refusing to burn incense to the emperor. The cults of emperor and Artemis were so commercially and politically interwoven that one could scarcely turn in any direction without meeting their faceless and impersonal pressures or compulsions. Imprisonment could be in a black pit without hope of light, or it could be in a decent room where he was allowed pen and paper.

Perhaps imprisonment meant peace. His "prison" letters, *Colossians, Philippians,* and *Philemon,* reflect a certain composure. In his letters, this compassionate bold man was able to penetrate to the heart of a matter with

an uncommon sureness. His patience, his Jewish persist-
ence, his experience, his love for these babes who were
ready only for gruel, his joy in the friends who grew
to be men—as did those in Philippi—his tongue-lash-
ings when all else had failed, were the sum of his
strength.

The discordant sounds which had come from Corinth
—almost from the moment of his departure—had increased in their pathetic shrillness. They demanded all
his skill and the widest range of his compassion. Corinthians, Ephesians, and Galatians were all shaped and
battered by a world from which old virtues had fled and
new expediencies filled their places thinly. Once there
had been a glory in Greece and perhaps even an innocence
in Asia, but the world which Christianity was challenging was like an arena where insatiable and terrible games
were played for an emperor whose authority controlled
every act and guarded every exit.

Paul was faced by the fact that the Corinthians had
taken the redemptive power of Christianity and with
a Greek cynicism tried to translate natural and unnatural
lusts into variations of Christian virtues. The love-feasts,
when Christians sat down together in memory of Jesus
and his love, had become displays of rich against poor,
of drunkenness and debauchery. Paul, buttressed by the
great morality of Judaism and made into a human being
by the transcendant challenge of Christianity, knew that
the fruits of the spirit could only be seen as steadfast
moral virtues. If this simple equation was not recognized,

then Christianity was no better than the Greek mysteries which represented quintessential ideals.

Without the deepest and most profound sense of love, all Christian protestations were no better than sounding brass or a tinkling cymbal. "Though I may have the gift of prophecy and understand all mysteries, though I may have all faith so that I can remove mountains and have not love I have nothing. Though I bestow all my goods to feed the poor and though I give my body to be burned, and have not love it profiteth me nothing."

Love is very patient, very kind. Love is without jealousy. Love is slow to expose, eager to believe the best, filled with hope.

Love never comes to an end.

It is a surpassing letter, the measure of the man's greatness.

He wrote some of it in verse so that it could be committed to memory. He took account of all their problems: one of the elders, a woman, wished to know if they should buy the sacrificial meat, sold in the public markets but bringing a profit to the temples of Aphrodite and Apollo? Should they take law cases to the civil courts? How should women dress in the churches which were not public places but private dwellings? How far should ecstatic speaking be allowed?

His answers were brilliant. Many of the hazards he dealt with were timeless, inherent in human behavior, but others were endemic to that vast prison house of the pagan world and, if not handled properly, could set awry the imperative balance of Christian life. Spiritual revelation, in one scale, must always be balanced and confirmed by moral values and conduct in the other.

It is hard to measure the weight he bore, caring for the churches. To these Corinthians he said with a bitter irony, "Five times have I received at the hands of the Jews the forty lashes less one. Three times I have been beaten with rods; once I was stoned. Three times I have been shipwrecked; a night and a day I have been adrift at sea; on frequent journeys in danger from rivers, danger from robbers, danger from my own people, danger from Gentiles, danger in the city, danger in the wilderness, danger at sea, danger from false brethren, in toil and hardship, through many a sleepless night, in hunger and thirst, in cold and exposure . . ." But his heaviest punishment was "the daily pressure upon me of my anxiety for all the churches. Who is weak and I am not weak? Who is made to fall and I am not indignant . . . What do you wish? Shall I come to you with a rod, or with love in a spirit of gentleness?" Even then he comforted them, ". . . For who shall separate us from the love of God? Shall tribulation or distress or persecutions or nakedness or peril or sword? Nay, in all these things we are more than conquerors through him that loved us."

The dangers which increased for him can only be conjectured. They could be dangers which grew out of the nature of this city and the constant refusal of the Christians to accommodate themselves to its restrictions. The ability of small communities of Christians to create large commotion inspires one's awe. On the other hand, we know that Paul gained powerful friends both in the basilica—"among the household of Caesar"—and among the Asiarchs. If *Romans* 16 is addressed to the Ephesians, as many scholars believe, we know the names of those he trusted among the Jews and Greeks. They were people of no small account, men and women whose houses served as churches.

But the prime danger lay in his constant reiteration that gods made with hands had no power. The great Artemis represented the powers of natural force in her original guise of black stone. But she had also assumed the characteristics of Cybele the Great Mother, of Hecate the goddess of destruction and the underworld, and of Artemis, goddess of moon, tides, and madness. Under her feet were the gold and vaults of Asia. Yet these Christians, without rhetoric or wild cries or immolation, denied her power as simply as they ate or walked or slept or abode in their good works, and this released many Asians from a great fear. But it inflamed the city. The people in the streets gave him peace one day and war the next. They would call after him obscenely or hail him with shouts, or they would have it both ways, hopping on one foot and shouting "Oh, Jesus! Oh, Artemis!"

For a time the Christian challenge could be muted by cymbals, pipes, and shouts but not forever. When the attack on the Christians came it held no surprise—except that it had been deferred for so long.

In every street of the city were those who lived and fed on the goddess; most dependent of all were the silversmiths, for they made the amulets and holy trinkets as well as the great statues given by rich men to the temple.

A silversmith called Demetrius raised the first cry, "Men, you know that from this business we have our wealth. And you see and hear that not only at Ephesus but almost throughout all Asia this Paul has persuaded and turned away a considerable company of people, saying that gods made with hands are not gods. And there is danger not only that this trade of ours may come into disrepute but also that the temple of the Great Goddess Artemis may count for nothing and that she may even be deposed from her magnificence, she whom all Asia and the world worship."

The men who heard him were filled with such alarm that they ran into the streets and raised the cry of warning: "Great is Artemis of the Ephesians!"

The cry was like a firebell. The people who lived in the streets caught up the warning. It rose shrilly to the basilica and to the palace of the Asiarch. It was heard in alleys and in the weaving shed of Aquila. Some cried one thing and some cried another, many did not know why they were crying and so cried the more.

Paul's friends heard the cries. The synagogue heard the cries. The governing assembly of Ephesus heard the cries.

Two Christians, Gaius and Aristarchus of Macedonia, were recognized and seized by the crowd which dragged them into the theatre.

Paul was determined to reach them. But his friends held him forcibly until stronger persuasion could be summoned. Asiarchs, who were friends, sent and begged him not to venture into the theatre.

The theatre, looking out over the sea, held twenty-five thousand people. Men, swarming up the steep sides or climbing up the seats, were shouting one thing and then another, many not knowing why they had come together or the reason for their shouts.

For two hours they swarmed and shouted, "Great is Artemis of the Ephesians!" One has a sense that the uprising was directed and controlled by a cunning hand— experienced perhaps in allowing dangerous emotions to exhaust themselves without too much damage to the community. At a crucial point, the town clerk, who presided at the governing assemblies, appeared before them, quieting them with the succinct reminder that the city of Ephesus was a linchpin in the structure of empire, carrying the honorific title bestowed upon it by Caesar of "Temple-keeper of the Great Artemis and of the sacred stone that fell from the sky."

"Seeing then that these things cannot be contradicted, you ought to be quiet and do nothing rash. For you have brought these men here who are neither sacrilegious nor blasphemers of our goddess. If therefore Demetrius and the craftsmen with him have a complaint against anyone, the courts are open, and there are Proconsuls. Let them bring charges against one another. But if you seek anything about other matters, it shall be settled in the regular assembly. For we are in danger of being charged with rioting today, there being no cause that we can give to justify this commotion."

This is a remarkable speech, spoken by a small great man, whatever his motives.

Gaius and Aristarchus went home unharmed.

That night Paul gathered together his friends and spoke to them. It seemed as though he always heard the great din of opposition as a trumpet call of God. The weaver in him now wished to test the texture of the churches. He had already sent Titus to Corinth where trouble was mounting and Paul's authority abused, Epaphras to Colossae, Timothy and Erastus to Macedonia. Into all this going and coming he had woven the gathering of funds for Jerusalem which would be the tangible evidence of a brotherhood of strength. Now he knew more deeply than ever that the bond between all Christian communities must be confirmed so that they could not be picked off one by one.

The resilience of this man was beyond measure. He was incapable of accepting defeat. Despair, yes; fear, self-doubt, but never defeat.

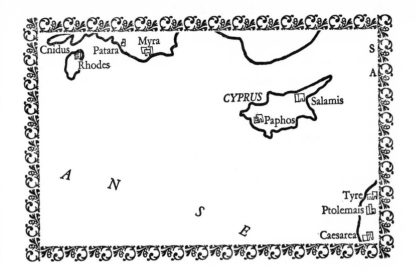

Cnidus Patara Myra S A

CYPRUS Salamis Paphos

A N S E

Tyre Ptolemais Caesarea

13

MACEDONIA, RHODES, CAESAREA

Without Were Fightings
Within Were Fears

Paul went up the coast to Troas where Titus was to join him. He waited but Titus did not come. There was no peace in his spirit, "because I found not Titus my brother; taking my leave, I went thence into Macedonia." He was exhausted. "Without were fightings, within were fears."

But in Macedonia he found Timothy. These churches in Thessalonia, Beroea, and Philippi were his gift from God. Why they had increased so steadily, met their afflictions with such composure, kept free of turmoil and factions, is hard to say. Perhaps the women of Philippi had a special gift of steadiness; perhaps the men Paul sent to walk with the new Christians—Luke, Silas, Timothy—had the gift of inspiration.

The churches of Macedonia were bitterly poor, but this was nothing uncommon considering the poor men and slaves who composed them. They seemed unaware of any restrictions, however, unperturbed by the hostility around them. "Out of a severe test of affliction, their abundance of joy and their extreme poverty have overflowed in a wealth of liberality on their part."

They immediately gave what they had to the fund he was gathering for Jerusalem. For five years they had given to him also for his journeys and his keep, although he had not wanted it, looking instead to his own hands. (Sometime, in these years, it is believed that Paul received a legacy. If, indeed, his family was wealthy in Tarsus a death may have left him an heir. In any event, there were unmistakable signs of easement from this time on.)

The Macedonians reassured him profoundly. Paul could draw for a long time on one measure of confidence. And Titus reached him presently with news so reassuring that Paul poured out his joy in a letter to the church in Corinth. The letter rang with the profound insight which had guided him for so long: rules, codes, priestcraft and "dispensations of death" had to yield to the splendor and brightness of the Christ within. "We are very bold, not like Moses who put a veil over his face so that the Israelites might not see the end of the fading splendor. But their minds were hardened; for to this day when they read the old covenant, that same veil remains unlifted because only through Christ is it taken away . . . But when a man turns to the Lord the veil is removed. Now the Lord is the Spirit and where the Spirit of the Lord is, there is liberty. And we all, with unveiled face, reflecting the glory of the Lord, are being changed into his likeness from glory unto glory . . . For God who commanded the light to shine out of darkness has shined in our hearts, to give the light of the knowledge of the glory of God in the face of Christ . . . From now on, therefore, we regard no one from a human point of view. Even though we once regarded Christ from a human point of view, we regard him thus no longer. Therefore if any man is in Christ he is a new creation, the old has passed away, behold all things are become new."

He was too experienced in human behavior to believe that quarreling and jealousy, anger and slander might not spring out again when he appeared, but he hoped that he himself would have the wisdom and hardihood to control it. He sent Titus and "two brethren" ahead of him to Corinth to make final collection of the fund which for Paul had such symbolic meaning. Generosity of brother to brother wove a garment that covered them all. Generosity from one church to another, if given, as the Macedonians did, out of a wealth of liberality, dissolved jealousy and encouraged reconciliation.

In the winter of 56, Paul himself came to Corinth— not over the mountains which would be closed by snow, but by caique which sailing close to the shore could make the journey even when black clouds rushed down from the mountains and the sea became the color of iron.

Sitting in the pale sunshine of Corinth he could feel himself on the threshold of Rome. Cross the narrow strip of Adriatic and he would stand in Italy. Italy filled his thoughts.

For years there had been a community of Christians in Rome, Peter's flock. Though many had been scattered by Claudius' decree, others had managed to remain and their numbers had grown in quiet ways. The church in Rome knew Paul only by reputation, and not all the reputation was good. Thinking so intently of Rome, knowing that he must link all in one bond of love, he wrote a letter to the church in Rome. He began by giving thanks—as he always did; gratitude was essential to Paul—for those who had made their lives anew for Christ. One can indeed only approach God, he wrote, through the mediation of Christ—through that transformed spiritual sense which is the mind of Christ.

Here was a man who learned from all—"I am debtor both to the Greeks and to the Barbarians, both to the wise and to the unwise"—and his obligation had no end.

He was moved to attack the society of the world in stinging and explicit terms, for Christians whether Jews or Gentiles were no better than their relation to the world about them. It was a letter rich in his own experience. Christ-compassion and forgiveness were the only answers to the curses and penalties of law, whether Jewish or Roman, and in this world of blind despair and helplessness, Jesus' promise that God is Love stood as the one hope. This fact must be a point of transcendant faith, for in the world of complex and malicious corruptibility or of fixed and remorseless law, whether of Jews or of Romans, the Christian's duties to himself, his brethren, and the world in which he lived must be acknowledged without dissimulation. "Let love be genuine; hate what is evil, hold fast to what is good. Never flag in zeal, be aglow with the Spirit, serve the Lord. Rejoice in your hope, be patient in tribulation, be constant in prayer. Bless them which persecute you: bless and curse not. Rejoice with them that do rejoice, and weep with them that weep. Live in harmony with one another . . . Repay no one evil for evil, but take thought for what is noble in the sight of all. Beloved, never avenge yourselves, but leave it to God. Do not be overcome by evil but overcome evil with good. Owe no man anything but to love one another . . . for love is the fulfilling of the law."

He enjoined tolerance as the measure of this love; he extoled orderliness and respect for civil authority. In many respects this letter to the Romans is the most remarkable of Paul's letters, for he leavens almost every aspect of the inner and the outer life with his wisdom and knowledge.

Perhaps if he had sailed to Rome and Spain in the spring of this year Christian history might have been different, but he was determined to keep to his plans: he would sail from Corinth to Syria with the Greek delegates to Jerusalem: Sopater, Aristarchus, Secundus, Gaius, Timothy, and the delegates of Asia, Tychicus and Trophimus. On the point of sailing, however, he heard of

a plot against his life and perhaps against the money
which he carried. It had all the signs of political murder
—and indeed with Nero as new emperor the desperation
of Judea had increased with his megalomania.

They left the ship abruptly and boarded one going up
the coast to Macedonia. He celebrated Passover in Philippi instead of in Jerusalem as he had intended, and then
he and his friends crossed the narrow sea to Troas. In
Troas was now a church and a young man, Eutychus,
whom he raised from the dead.

From Troas the vessel went down the ancient and
vibrant coast of Aeolia and Ionia where the old world
was still strong enough to resist the new.

Paul, who wasted few impressions, who turned his life
and knowledge into metaphors, would have seen this
eastern shore in all its vividness. In April on the Aegean,
the scent of flowers and the sound of music affirmed
once more the round of life reborn and undefeated. Here
was the theme of all he spoke and did, and though this
world was pagan, the people were men and women.

At this time of year the wind blew from the north
until the end of day, when it fell into a dead quiet. Each
day the ship ran before the wind until the sunset. At
night they lay in harbor, for even with a favorable wind,
coastal boats avoided night runs, since reefs were unmarked and there were no lighthouses. From Mitylene,
the chief town in the island of Lesbos, they came opposite to Chios, the birthplace of Homer, and from thence
past Samos and the fierce headland of Mycale where the

temple of Poseidon cast out and drew back the sudden black clouds and capricious winds. They passed Ephesus gleaming in the sun.

When they put in at Miletus to unload and load the ship again, Paul sent a messenger back to Ephesus to bring the elders of the church to him. It took a day and a half for the messenger to cross the gulf to Priene and cross the hills to Ephesus and return by boat with the elders.

On the third day they talked together—Paul and the men and women of the church in Ephesus. He told them his fears, for now he guessed that plots against his life were part of the political turmoil against Rome. These were times of iron and fire and sudden death. He might not see these friends again. He said to them, "Shepherd the church of Jesus which he bought with his blood. For I know that after my departure, grievous wolves will enter in among you, sparing not the flock. Therefore be alert, remembering that for three years I did not cease night or day to admonish everyone with tears. And now I commend you to God and to the word of his grace which is able to build you up and to give you the inheritance. You yourselves know that these hands ministered to my necessities and to those who were with me. In all things I have shown you that by so toiling one must help the weak, remembering the words of the Lord Jesus, 'It is more blessed to give than to receive.' "

Then he knelt down with them and prayed. They wept and he wept with them, and they exchanged the kisses of love and farewell. When the evening came they brought him to the ship which was now waiting for the wind at sunrise.

Even though he might not see them again, Ephesus would be, after Philippi, his dearest church.

As they went across the sea at dawn, the open-roofed temple to Apollo on the headland of Didyme caught the first light. It was the largest temple in the world, and still unfinished. Menelaus had hung his shield in the temple and the oracle here was very pure and lofty—but the church in Ephesus was a greater temple, made without hands.

They came by straight run to Cos, sacred to Aesculapius and the arts of medicine, and the day after they reached Rhodes, that is, the Rose, called by some the most beautiful city in the world.

The statue of Apollo, one of the seven wonders of ancient times, lay broken below the waters of the bay. Paul saw it, as Pliny did in the same year. It had been a hundred feet high, with a staircase running the length of the body, the thumb too large to clasp in a man's arm. Pliny wrote, "Even as it lies it excites our wonder and imagination." In its eyes, it was said, beacon lights had been kindled for the ships at sea, yet now it lay, as all these gods would lie, quite helpless and forlorn.

They passed to Patara on the Lycian coast where fine rain fell each morning like dew, and cirrus clouds floated higher and higher, the vanishing hoofs of Pegasus, it was said. The Lycians were strange people of unknown origin who had resisted the Greeks and Romans.

As the ship moved down the coast toward Myra, the

cedar and juniper woods of the highlands brought a faint fragrance when the wind blew from the east. In rocky clefts between the trees ancient tombs held a long watch above the sea.

If Paul had had reason or temper to look back into time, he would have seen all this coast as a vast transparency for ages past and gods forsaken.

Myra was a great port for grain ships from Egypt and North Africa, bound for Rome; here too ships from Syria took on cargo or unloaded their vessels. Myra was the home of the sailors' god—he who was later transformed into St. Nicholas of Myra, patron of sailors—and prayers and sacrifices were offered before the unchartered run across the open sea. The prevailing winds were westerly, and blew with the steadiness of trade winds; a direct run to Syria or to Egypt carried less risk than did the journey which hugged the coast where the reefs were unmarked.

Cyprus lay to their left and with a steady wind they reached Tyre on the Syrian coast the next day.

The vessel remained in Tyre for seven days while it unloaded and was refitted.

Strabo claimed that Tyre had taller buildings than Rome and greater filth. For a thousand years the city's prosperity had come from its dyed textiles, and the perpetual stench of the dyeing vats filled the air.

Christians lived in Tyre. During these seven days Paul's party searched them out, and men who had been strangers one moment were brothers the next.

They begged Paul not to go to Jerusalem. Terrible

and bloody battles had been fought in Samaria and
Galilee. Men had been crucified by the hundreds. Zealots
were turning in desperation to the Assassins. Roman soldiers did not move through the hills unless fully armed,
and Paul would not be armed as the Romans were.

Paul knew that he could not listen, and when "the
day ended, they all with wives and children brought us
on our way till we were outside the city, and kneeling
down on the beach we prayed and bade one another farewell."

At Ptolemais which was their last stop before Caesarea
they again found men and their wives and children who
were Christians, and who loved what Christianity had
done to their lives. What better encouragement could a
man like Paul have, going into God knows what danger?

In Caesarea lived Philip, who had been an apostle of
Jesus. He welcomed Paul and the delegates bearing the
collection, and they stayed in his house. It was the round-
ing of a circle. In the days of Saul the avenger, Philip
had been driven from Jerusalem and he had carried the
first message to the Gentiles.

In Philip's house the warnings of Tyre were repeated.
The country was on the verge of warfare.

The new procurator Felix was a monster of vice. He
lived in Caesarea in a state of siege. Though dealing ruth-
lessly with the Jewish brigands in the mountains—who
were patriots to the Jews—he had not been able to deal
with the Daggermen who struck in full daylight in the
midst of the city.

"Festivals were their special seasons," wrote Josephus,

"when they would mingle with the crowd, carrying short daggers concealed under their clothes with which they stabbed their enemies. Then when they fell the murderers joined in the cries of indignation and, through this plausible behavior, were never discovered." They assassinated "Jonathan the high priest; after his death there were numerous daily murders. The panic created was more alarming than the calamity itself; everyone as on the battlefield hourly expected death. Men kept watch at a distance on their enemies and would not trust even their friends when they approached. Yet, even while their suspicions were aroused and they were on their guard, they fell; so swift were the conspirators and so crafty in eluding detection."

Josephus does not say that to many Jews the Dagger-men were heroes, for their weapons were directed against those who, like the High Priest, had joined with Rome.

The Romans, watching from Antony's Tower which overlooked the Temple, and from their patrols around the city, were even more concerned by the "deceivers and imposters" who used the words of divine inspiration to foster revolution.

An Egyptian Jew, who had the reputation of a prophet, gathered a following of thousands—Josephus says 30,000, Luke says 4,000. In any event he led them through the wilderness to the outskirts of Jerusalem and set his garrison on the Mount of Olives, planning to take the city by storm and destroy the Romans.

An informer betrayed him to Felix, but the Egyptian

escaped with some of his followers. Most however were killed or taken prisoner.

"But no sooner were these disorders reduced than the inflammation, as in a sick man's body, broke out again in another quarter." Many were incited to revolt and promised tokens of divine guidance; violent threats were offered to all who submitted to Roman rule. These insurrectionists were at this moment—when Paul waited in Caesarea—scattered in companies through the country, terrorizing Roman adherents, looting the homes of the wealthy, killing, and burning villages. "The frenzy was felt throughout all Judea," said Josephus, "and every day saw this war being fanned into fiercer flame."

The present High Priest was in a collusive pact with Felix, and the only hope of preserving some glory in Israel lay with the Pharisees who were crying out like Isaiah and Jeremiah for a return to prophetic vision.

Paul was not rash but he believed that God's plan for him moved within its own context of events.

As he was about to set out, an old prophet named Agabus came down from Jerusalem through the mountains of Samaria, entered Philip's house and without a word took the girdle from Paul's waist and bound it about his own hands and feet.

"So shall the Jews at Jerusalem bind the man that owns this girdle and deliver him into the hands of the Gentiles."

The simplicity of this ancient gesture and archaic warning chilled the hearts of all his friends and of those who had come with him from Greece and Asia.

They begged Paul not to go to Jerusalem, for what fate might have been designed for him who saw the kingdom of salvation as somewhat larger than a single nation?

But, he answered, "Why do you weep and break my heart? for I am ready not only to be bound but to die in Jerusalem for the name of the Lord Jesus."

He had come in harmony, and the gifts he carried to the church in Jerusalem would be given in harmony. Jerusalem meant "the abode of harmony." Paul, that mercurial man of deep passions, had all his Christian life wished to separate the chaff from the wheat and bind the wheat together as an act of peace without equal. If an act as symbolic as this offering to the brethren in Jerusalem was his last harmonizing gesture, he had faith that God would lift it up. He had never moved until the spirit gave direction, and he had come this far by that direction.

He was so clear and sure that the others were obliged to say, "The will of the Lord be done."

The Caesarean Christians went with them half-way, and arranged that they should break their journey in the safe house of an old disciple, Mnason of Cyprus, for in the mountains brigands posed as patriots and patriots as brigands, and danger lay in every fold of the hills.

The season was beautiful and Pentecost was joyful; when the holy city came upon their sight across the valley no man, Greek, Asian, or Jew, could stay unmoved. It symbolized all that was most noble in the journey of the soul.

The Temple stood high on Mount Moriah looking across the Kidron Valley to the Mount of Olives. The Roman fortress of Antony kept its iron watch beside the Temple. On the western hill the palace of Herod completed the triumvirate which held such a dazzling and worldly grip on Jewish inspiration.

Around the holy city were the tents and watch fires of the pilgrims who had come from all the lands of the Diaspora for the holy season. Paul entered the city with courage; he could not fancy that he would go unnoticed. Pilgrims were in Jerusalem from all the synagogues which he had split in two: Pisidian Antioch and Lystra, Syrian Antioch, Cyprus, Thessalonica, Beroea, Corinth, Ephesus. Within the city were his high priestly enemies who had kept alive their obsessive hate. Yet to Paul, danger and the future went hand in hand.

He took his flock of Gentiles, his Greeks and his half-Jews, with the offering gathered from the Gentile world, and went to James. The confrontation excites one's sensibilities; one may give too much or too little to this strange enigmatic figure, this man called The Just, who had acquired an hieratic position because of his relation to Jesus. His devotion to the Law, his exemplary behavior as a Jew, had permitted the Christians of Jerusalem to assume a position of such neutral tones that they could remain indistinguishable if they chose.

In a city which trembled day and night with political violence, such a skillful blending of externals may have preserved the life of the Nazarene community, but in a deeper more subjective sense it corrupted that innocent exaltation which had been capable of seeing its great faith unkilled, untombed.

Now James and the elders received the offerings. Paul gave an accounting of his ministry. Thanks were given, courtesies exchanged. Then an old fear was put as an arch over the occasion. "You see, brother Paul, how many thousands there are among the Jews who believe on the Lord Jesus; they are all zealous of the law; they have been told about you that you teach the Jews who are among the gentiles to forsake Moses, telling them not to circumcise their children or observe the customs. What then is to be done? They will certainly hear that you have some."

What James was saying was clear, but what he left unsaid was also clear. *Pilgrims have a gift for excess. The flax is waiting for the flame.* The febrile patriotism of a desperate idealistic people could be turned against the Christians by one incautious act.

The Christians, however, had a simple act of piety by which they might protect themselves.

"We have four men who are under a vow. Take these men and purify yourselves at the completion of the vow. Thus all will know that there is nothing in what they have been told about you, but that you yourself live in observance of the law."

Paul, a Pharisee of the Pharisees, knew very well what this entailed. The completion of a Nazarite vow was an ancient ritual, set down by Moses. Supporting a poorer brother in the discharge of his vow was an acknowledged act of piety. It lay within the great definition of love, and

required Paul to share the last days of penitence, to lie on
the floor of the Nazarite chamber within the Court of
Israel, to fulfill all the rites of purification, addressing
no man, holding his thought to prayer. Then on the
seventh day he must stand with the five men in the Dock
of Atonement to endure the formal humiliations and
mockery of the men of Israel and be exposed—he, Paul
—to the knife of a Daggerman.

It could be his death sentence.

Paul had come to Jerusalem for harmony. If this was
the token of reconciliation, he agreed.

The friends who were with him from the Greek and
Asian worlds were helpless to protect him, for at the
gate of the inner court was a tablet written in Greek:
"No foreigner may enter the space within the barrier
and the wall which is around the temple: whoever is
arrested has brought himself the penalty which is death."
Among them only Timothy was not a foreigner in Israel.

Paul fulfilled all the obligations of the vow. On the
seventh day he stood in the Dock of Atonement. The
signal cry went up, " 'Men of Israel, help! This is the
man who is teaching the people everywhere against the
people and the law and this place; moreover he brought
Greeks into the Temple and he has defiled this holy place.'

"The whole city was roused and the people ran together. They seized Paul and dragged him out of the
Temple and the gates were shut."

They flung him onto the paving stones of the Court
of the Gentiles to beat him to death. The pupils of rabbis,
sitting at their masters' feet in Solomon's Porch, the

sellers of doves and lambs, the changers of money, and all the idle who made their gestures of piety by kicking their heels in the outer court, ran this way and that, in horror, compassion, greedy excitement.

Violence within the precincts of the Temple was a desperate commonplace. Rumors fluttered and flew up like pigeons. The Temple guards, who were very strict and exact with their whips, could reach only the edge of the crowd at the heart of which a man was being killed. On the watchtowers of the fortress the Roman sentries began to strike their shields with their swords.

The Romans were very precise in their judgment of riot. They interfered only when the level had reached the extreme point of danger. The tribune, with his guards and officers, now ran down the steps which led from the fortress into the Court of the Gentiles and, in the way known only to Romans, brought an end to the killing of Paul.

The tribune ordered Paul chained to two soldiers and his officers demanded to know who this man was and what he had done. So many cried out the answers that the tribune named Claudius Lysias commanded that Paul be carried into the fortress.

This drove the people quite mad. They surged after the Romans with such violence that the soldiers were obliged to lift Paul off his feet to a place of safety. A thousand voices cried, "Destroy him!"

The battered and bloody man cried to the tribune, "May I speak to you?"

Claudius Lysias was astonished into an ejaculation.

"You speak Greek? Are you not that Egyptian who recently threatened the city of Jerusalem and escaped into the wilderness with four thousand Assassins?"

"I am a Jew, from Tarsus in Cilicia, a citizen of no mean city. I beg you let me speak to the people."

Nothing quiets a mob more quickly than curiosity. To see Paul stand there and summon quiet with his chained hands was a great subduer.

Paul trusted the gift of speech. It was the best way he knew to reconcile the heart and mind. But the silence was the silence of bitter and angry men, the silence of armored soldiers, the silence of the priests and, one ventures, of the High Priest himself who had a private window which gave him access to all that went on within the Temple. Perhaps Paul reached too many hearts and minds, for suddenly the cries began again, "Away with such a fellow from the earth: he is not fit to live!"

Claudius Lysias did not understand the words, but he understood the new pitch of violence and the ancient gesture of clothes ripped and dust poured on the head. He gave the command to bring Paul into the fortress, and bolt the doors, and question him under the lash.

The scourge was metal tipped. When applied by an experienced hand it could cut a man's veins and lay bare his entrails.

Paul was not ready to die. As the soldiers forced him into a stooping position, binding him with thongs to the whipping post, he said to the officer in command, "Is it lawful for you to scourge a man who is a Roman citizen, and uncondemned?"

The centurion was aghast. If there was a perfection in life, guarded by all the force of the Caesars, it was this citizenship. Many a man had given all his lifetime earnings to die under its blessing. The centurion went in agitation to Claudius Lysias saying, "What are you about to do? This man is a Roman citizen!"

Claudius Lysias came without delay. "Are you a Roman?"

"I am."

"With a great sum obtained I my freedom!"

"I was freeborn."

An extraordinary exchange, laying bare the greatness of Rome and the fears of life, and yet, by the insight of Paul, lifting a human condition into a spiritual statement of freedom.

Now Claudius Lysias, who had been so confused in his routine assumptions, looked about for sharp certain facts. When the Temple hierarchs laid a formal charge against Paul, Claudius Lysias caught a glimmer of light. He did not know that the long, coiling, tenacious, orthodox hatred of this man Paul was unwinding itself in the charge, that the priests saw a mortal enemy in Paul, saw a renegade, a man who had appeared in synagogue after synagogue splitting them apart with his false Messiah, a Roman who called himself a Jew, a betrayer of Israel, a blasphemer, a man to be feared more than the dead Jesus.

To Lysias Paul was simply a Roman citizen for whom he was responsible—but a Roman who must answer the charge of starting a Jewish riot. Lysias required the Sanhedrin to meet in a part of the Temple where a Roman could be admitted. He himself brought Paul and set him before them.

It was not a trial, for the Sanhedrin had no jurisdiction over a Roman; it was an airing of charges. Lysias listened to the charges. Paul himself interpreted them as expedient and theological—indeed they could not have been charges of blasphemy or political riot for too many had seen Paul stand in the Dock of Atonement. This High Priest was more venal than most; presently he would be killed by a Daggerman. The corruption was eating its way through the priesthood; Sadducees were suborned.

Lysias concluded that no charges had been preferred —only a fist blow at Paul's mouth delivered by direction of the High Priest and a great falling-out in consequence between Pharisees and Sadducees, some of the Pharisees crying, "We find nothing wrong in this man!"

Claudius Lysias saw his Roman citizen once more in danger from violent men. He commanded his guards to force their way to the protection of Paul and bring him back to the fortress while he resolved what to do with this strange bird in his hand.

Paul, the man of vivid courage, heard that night a voice say to him, *Be of good cheer.*

Every sinew in his body still ached from the blows of Jews or of Romans.

As you have testified of me in Jerusalem so you will bear witness also at Rome.

It was enough to take away the pain.

Claudius Lysias was obliged, by the nature of his commission, to deliver Paul up the rungs of justice to the Roman Procurator in Caesarea. But he made the move in the dead of night because word came to him that more than forty patriots had bound themselves by an oath to kill Paul. Their plot was a devious one, enlisting the High Priest and members of the Council.

That evening Claudius Lysias called two of his centurions and said, "At the third hour of the night get ready two hundred soldiers with seventy horsemen and two hundred spearsmen to go as far as Caesarea. Also provide mounts for Paul to ride and bring him safely to Felix the governor."

This was a veritable army, and the size of the army has raised doubts in the minds of scholars.

But it was plain to Lysias that the country was in a turmoil. In the cities the power of armed patriots was increasing daily. In the countryside armed bands controlled the roads. The extraordinary tumult that had engulfed Paul suggested to Lysias that here was a man of some importance. The most casual inquiry disclosed that Paul led a well-organized religious cult, quasi-Jewish and legal. The Pharisees defended him. Claudius Lysias was not authorized to think too deeply about these matters; he was authorized to inform himself of facts and take appropriate action.

In the dead of the night the little army set out with this Paul, this inspired nuisance, this sublime troublemaker who caused riots in every city to which he came.

The Romans hated this country, and the country hated the Romans. The sound of an army passing must have shaken many out of their sleep. Lynx and jaguars and patriots could watch with night eyes. Antipatris which lay at the foot of the mountains was reached the next day. There the foot soldiers left to return to Jerusalem and the mounted guards brought Paul the rest of the way to Caesarea.

Paul now stood in a marble vestibule to Rome.

Caesarea had been brought into life by Herod the Great to please Caesar Augustus. Herod had built an artificial harbor to protect the ships, bound from Phoenicia to Egypt, from the stormy seas of this region. It had marble piers and on the waterfront were great twin statues of Augustus and Roma whose marble fingers beckoned to the ships at sea. When Caesarea became the capital of Roman Palestine the palace of the Herodian kings became the seat of the Procurators.

Paul was delivered into the care of Antonius Felix who read the letter of Lysias and looked at Paul with curiosity. He asked to what province his citizenship adhered and he said, "I will hear you when your accusers are also come." He ordered him lodged under guard in this great palace.

Paul looked with interest at Felix. This man was a synonym for vice.

He was also shrewd, able, and courageous in a world where courage was not always the virtue which led to preferment. He had been born a slave and brother to Pallas, the notorious favorite of Claudius Caesar. Pallas had brought his freedom and his brother's, dominated

Claudius with great ability, and became the second rich-est man in all antiquity (the first was Narcissus, Clau-dius' secretary of state and also a freedman).

Felix, with this powerful support, and "with all man-ner of cruelty and lust, exercised the functions of a prince with the disposition of a slave." These are Tacitus' words and indicate the aristocrat's disdain of a freedman rather than an objective appraisal of Felix' ability. Felix represented the new Rome where an old caste was dying and the Asians and Greeks whom Rome had enslaved were assuming the powers of administration, trade, and finance. Most of these Greeks and Asians were freedmen who retained their old servile manners as well as their hatred of masters.

Felix had worked with the Jews and against the Jews. He had been a friend to the Assassins and had led an army against them. Prisoners crucified by him lined the roads. Three times he led a Roman army against rebellions, including the rebellion of that Egyptian whom Lysias had confused with Paul. In these bloody ways, Felix had maintained an uneasy order.

Felix the freedman had married three times, each wife a princess, each princess seduced. His present wife was nineteen years old, an Herodian princess named Drusilla, who had been married to the king of nearby Emesa and taken from him with the help of a magician, a magician of Cyprus whom many scholars have wished to identify with Bar-Jesus.

Five days after Paul's arrival, Ananias the High Priest

and members of the Sanhedrin, and a lawyer named
Tertullus came down the mountains from Jerusalem
and laid their case before Felix.

Tertullus preferred the charges against "this pestilent
fellow, this mover of seditions among the Jews throughout the world, this ringleader of the sect of Nazarenes.
He has even tried to profane the Temple, but we seized
him and would have judged him according to our law
had not the chief captain Lysias come and with great
violence taken him out of our hands. You yourself will
be able to learn from him the truth of our accusations."

Tertullus' clients, sitting in a formal row against the
wall, looked sideways at the Procurator on his raised dais
and affirmed that this was true. When Felix pointed his
finger at Paul, Paul rose to defend himself. The defense
was composed and orderly. "I do most cheerfully answer
for myself." He made neither too much nor too little of
the matter. He demonstrated that their charges were
both impossible and illegal and that he could call on
many witnesses to support him.

Felix, with a Jewish wife, was not uninformed of
Jewish law, and he had some knowledge of the Christian
way. The hearing, preliminary to a larger process, required no verdict. He merely said, "When Lysias, the
tribune, comes down I will decide your case."

He gave orders that Paul should have some liberty and
free access to his friends.

The Christians of Caesarea were his friends. Philip,
Timothy, and Luke were also in Caesarea, as well as those
others who came and went at his bidding. Paul was

greatly concerned about the communities in Greece and Asia and presently sent Trophimus and Tychicus back to Asia and the Greeks to Greece. Luke and Timothy remained, it appears, and others came and went.

Lysias did not come down to Caesarea; the seasons passed; Felix sent for Paul many times and asked him questions of the Christ.

This custody held no danger except from tedium. Paul answered Felix without temporizing. He talked of justice and self-control and final judgments. This fascinated and alarmed Felix who had other judgments to consider—judgments of Paul's access to wealth, judgments of how large a bribe he might be able to extract.

One did not ask a bribe from a poor man. For this reason, and many other reasons contingent on his vendible soul, Felix sent often for Paul and talked with him for a long time.

There is no way of knowing what Paul felt about his confinement, but passionate, visionary, journeying men do not bear confinement well. Paul however had had a vision that he would preach in Rome and he had learned, long ago, that when the Spirit set his course the way became clear.

The seasons went by and the tensions of the country swelled into another armed revolt.

In Caesarea itself the Jewish portion of the city rose against the Greeks, claiming the city was theirs because Herod the Great had been a Jew. The Greeks disputed this, pointing to the statues that Herod had erected in honor of Augustus as proof that Herod had not designed the city for the Jews. "Daily the more venturesome in either camp would rush into combat," Josephus wrote, "for the older members of the Jewish community were incapable of restraining their turbulent partisans, and the Greeks considered it humiliating to give way to the Jews. The latter had the advantage of superior wealth and physical strength, the Greeks that of the support of the military, for the troops stationed here were mainly levied by the Romans from Syria and were always ready to lend aid to their compatriots."

Arrests and beatings only inflamed the Greeks or Jews. When at length an armed battle was fought in the city streets, a battle won by the Jews, Felix appeared in the market place and ordered them to lay down their arms. They refused and he ordered his troops to attack them. The streets, already running blood, were crimsoned again.

Still they fought. At last Felix sent the leaders of the Jews and Greeks to bring their quarrel before Nero. But in this way he brought about his own downfall, for the Jewish delegates accused him before Nero of duplicity.

For two years Felix had made no move in Paul's behalf or against him. Now he made a staggering effort to help himself up the slippery slope which armed patriots and embattled religionists kept beneath the feet of Roman procurators. With the Caesarean Jews building a strong case against him, Felix was in desperate need of an ingratiating action. In Paul he had a man against whom hatreds could be united. There is evidence that in Rome he handed to his successor a report hostile to Paul. Felix' successor, Porcius Festus, feeling the earth move under his feet as well, went to Jerusalem three days after his arrival in Palestine and immediately met with the High Priest and his supporters in the Council who informed him against Paul. They begged that Paul be sent to them, and few believed that Paul would reach Jerusalem alive. But Festus urged that they come to Caesarea and prefer their charges there. He promised he would not delay his judgment.

Festus was unlike Felix. He lacked Felix' malign and lively imagination; he was a prudent, honest man who might have administered the country ably had the situation not been chaos built on violence.

He felt no concern for Paul; his only concern was for peace in this wretched land. Within two weeks Paul stood in mortal danger.

The High Priest's charges had grown more violent with the passing of time, and linked with them now was the charge that Paul had offended the emperor.

Paul answered with spirit. Festus, still anxious to placate officialdom, said to him, "Will you go up to Jerusalem and there be tried on these charges before me?"

This, being translated, meant, "Will you return to the traps laid by the High Priest?"

True, Paul would still be a Roman citizen, but any hope of disinterested justice on the part of Rome would be hopelessly compromised by a verdict against him by the High Priest.

Will you go up to your death? Festus might have asked.

Paul answered, "I stand at Caesar's judgment seat where I should be judged. To the Jews I have done no wrong as you very well know. If I have done anything for which I deserve to die, I do not seek to escape death, but if there is nothing to their charges against me, no one can give me up to them. I appeal to Caesar!"

The ring of the words was, in time, heard in Ephesus, in Corinth, in Philippi, in the highlands of Galatia. *I challenge the ruler of the world to sustain my right to preach the awful daring of the Christ.*

Porcius Festus felt, perhaps, a profound relief. His foot, groping on the slimy slope, had found firm ground.

"Have you appealed unto Caesar? Unto Caesar you shall go."

14

ROME
Journey's End

Paul's sense of irony and his sense of vision found companionship in this imminence of Rome. He had not planned to come as a prisoner, but coming in such guise meant that every door would be opened straight to the gates of the city.

Festus put Paul and other prisoners into the custody of a centurion of the Augustan cohort named Julius who was bound for Rome. Julius was, it appears, a "peregrini," that is, an officer on detached duty belonging to the special corps, *princeps Peregrinorum.*

The status of the corps was unusual and honored. Its officers were couriers between the emperor and his provincial armies. They controlled the commissariat and were responsible for prisoners who, for one reason or another, were being sent to Rome.

Paul was allowed an attendant which made him a man of some consequence. Aristarchus of Thessalonica went with him and, by tradition, Luke since "we" is resumed in *Acts* at this point. Julius drew conclusions from this privileged position, treated Paul courteously, and gave him a large measure of freedom.

As for the other prisoners, who they were and how many is unknown. The arenas of Rome were beginning to make insatiable demand on the provinces for prisoners to be sacrificed at the games. Under Nero the demand reached charnal proportions.

Ships for Rome were more readily found in the ports along the Aegean than in Caesarea. The centurion and his prisoners sailed along the Asian coast, and Paul was allowed to go among his friends in Sidon "to refresh himself." They sailed past Cilicia and Pamphylia—all this world he knew so well—and at Myra found an Egyptian grain ship bound for Italy.

Egypt was the granary of the empire. Grain ships belonged to the imperial fleet and usually traveled in a large convoy. The ship found at Myra had, perhaps, put in for repairs, and from the government representative who sailed with the vessel—and was known euphoniously as the master of the ship—Julius had the right to requisition passage.

These vessels were great seagoing behemoths of high decks and high prows with the towering figure of a guardian goose at the stern. Geese had saved Rome; geese were sacred to Isis, and Isis was the guardian of ships.

They carried one great square mainsail and a smaller foresail on a short raked foremast and were able to dare the seas later in the season than the ordinary seagoing ships. But they were stately and clumsy like huge mammals which the world had outgrown.

The season for navigation was late, and violent storms were already raging up and down the Lycian coast, swelling the rivers and forming capricious currents. The Roman sea was officially closed to navigation between mid-September and March though exceptions were made for government business. A dread of the sea lived with all sailors. "Thy tacklings were loosed: they could not well strengthen their mast, they could not spread the sail; thus is the prey of a great spoil divided," Isaiah wrote centuries before, and a sailor knew what this meant in his bones and his soul.

Sailors lived by extra senses and by superstition and intuition which could not always be told apart, and by their skill with the winds. The Greeks, who hated and feared the sea, set their course by the Great Dipper. The Jews, who hated and feared the sea, set their course by the Little Dipper. In storm and on cloudy nights they cast all hope on the mercies of heaven. "He commandeth and raiseth the stormy wind, which lifteth up the waves thereof. They mount up to the heaven; they go down again to the depths; their soul is melted. They reel to and fro and stagger like a drunken man and are at their wits' end."

The Romans were bolder, as they were in most things which called for bone and muscle, but they had a great dread of the monsters which lurked in the deep and the terrible black desolate wastes when no stars appeared. The sacrifices that rose from the ship's altar morning and evening were their best hope for seeing them safely home.

The grain ship ran into the strong west winds of the autumn and was obliged to break for the open sea. As the winds grew perverse and the dangers increased, Crete loomed on their starboard side. They made their way into the harbor of Fair Havens to consider their plight. It was a harbor unsuited to such a large ship, but if they continued along the Cretan coast they would have to bear the full rage of a northwestern wind. The centurion Julius, as the ranking officer aboard, called a council of the captain, the ship master, and this notable man his prisoner—this traveler who knew the roads of Asia and Greece and the paths of the sea, who had been shipwrecked three times, adrift a night and a day on the deep. What did he counsel?

The captain and the ship master wished to chance the winds as far as Phoenix at the tip of Crete. They knew the dangers, but they also knew that after November 11 Phoenix would be closed and that Fair Havens offered an exposed and hazardous retreat.

But Paul opposed them. He matched his knowledge of the sea to theirs. His "lost years" in Tarsus may have familiarized him with Crete. If they went on, he said, "I perceive that the voyage will be with injury and much loss not only of the cargo and the ship but also of our lives."

The final decision was the prerogative of the ranking officer and Julius resolved to go on. When a south wind sprang up—the wind they needed—the anchor was weighed and they sailed close to shore.

But in the open bay beyond Cape Matala, a north-eastern gale swept without warning down from the mountains. Such a tempest was the dread of all sailors. The clumsy great ship with its two sails was flung into the troughs of the sea. It could not face the wind and so they could only lurch forward hoping to maneuver as the wind died. But the wind increased.

Now, tossing, reeling, the shore out of sight, the typhonic wind was driving them straight toward the African shore and the quicksands of the Syrtis.

They had not been able to slacken the sail but if they did not ease the pressure the mast would break and the ship be shaken to pieces and themselves all cast into the sea.

The sailors knew that their only hope lay in reaching the smooth waters of a bay and to do so they must control the ship in some fashion. They dropped sea anchors of stones and weights to retard their drift and lowered the sails to attempt the act of "clawing" for safety, allowing just enough sail to keep the ship's prow to the wind.

Prisoners and crew worked together in the howling wind, undergirding the ship. To save the strain on the timbers, ropes were passed around the hull of the ship from stem to stern and tightened by all arms pulling together. Through these desperate maneuvers they reduced their helplessness so that the ship drifted and was not driven. But the danger of sprung timbers increased with every wave that smashed against the hull, and when, at dawn, the tempest was still raging, crew and passengers threw overboard most of the cargo.

On the third day, still at the mercy of the storm, they jettisoned the ship's fittings and equipment, and the mainyard, which was now useless and a danger.

From the straining of the ship they knew that leaks had sprung, yet they dared not cut away the mast for it alone stood between them and the omnipotent sea.

Neither sun nor stars appeared in many days. With the terrors of darkness upon them they surrendered all hope. Curse the malign sea, and die! But Paul had, in the stillness of his closed eyes, seen a vision of life. He had seen that as man's faith in the divine order of life was used without limit, so was it increased without bound.

He came forward in the teeth of the wind and said to them, "You should have listened to me, but now I bid you take heart. For there shall be no loss of life among you, but only of the ship. There stood by me this night an angel of God, to whom I belong and whom I serve, and he said, 'Do not be afraid, Paul; you must stand before Caesar, and lo, God has granted you all those who sail with you.' So be of good cheer, for I have faith in God that it will be as I have been told."

Then he added, perhaps with a little irony since his advice had not been heeded before, "But we shall have to run on to some island."

For fourteen days they drifted across the open sea, sick, exhausted, and terrified. On the fourteenth night the sailors heard what the landsmen did not: the faint sound of breakers. The weak and the sick sprang into life. They took soundings and found twenty fathoms. A little further they sounded again and found fifteen fathoms. With the strong wind still blowing, fearing they would dash against the unmarked reef, they cast four anchors out of the stern to turn the prow to the land, and then they prayed for the day to arrive.

Now that hope had come, some men could not endure these last hours. They said they would lower the boat in order to anchor the bow, but they really planned to escape.

Paul said to Julius the centurion, "Unless these men stay on the ship, you cannot be saved."

There was nothing mysterious in his words; a ship of this size could not be beached unless every man took a hand. The centurion commanded his soldiers to cut the ropes of the boat. Then Paul begged them all to take food. "Today is the fourteenth day you have con-

tinued in suspense and without food. I pray you eat
for your health, for not a hair is to perish from the head
of any of you."

He took food before them all, and gave thanks to
God, and ate. All the others took heart, ate, and were
very much strengthened. By daybreak they were able
to lighten the ship even more, throwing out the last
of the grain.

When the day came, the sailors did not recognize the
land, but they saw a bay with a beach, so they cast off
the anchors, loosened the ropes that tied the rudder, and
hoisted the sail. The ship was weak however and the
men were faint and the wind drove them onto a shoal.
The bow was stuck fast, and, in the violence of the
waves, the stern splintered and broke.

The soldiers cried out to Julius that the prisoners
must be killed lest any swim away and escape. But
Julius knew now that under all circumstances he must
save Paul. He ordered each man who could swim to
throw himself into the sea, and those who could not
swim to seek help from the others or keep afloat on
broken planks of the ship.

In the cold and the heavy rain, they stumbled onto
the beach and when the count, was taken, not a single
man had been lost.

They learned that the island was Malta. They had
drifted over six hundred miles.

All sailors knew Malta but seldom as castaways. Her
great harbor lay on the other side of the island. Malta was
under Roman authority, being attached to the province

of Sicily. The Maltese were an ancient people, Semites
of Phoencian extraction, their language a dialect of the
Punic.

They were also a kind people and set out food and
warmth for these shipwrecked, water-soaked, hungry,
and injured men. All things considered, their curiosity
was surely admissible. When Paul, helping to gather
sticks, was struck by a viper, they set up a cry, "No
doubt this man is a murderer who, though he has escaped the sea, is struck down by Dike the goddess of
justice and vengeance!"

Though he shook off the viper, they waited with
great expectation for him to fall down in convulsions.
They waited all through the meal and when they saw
that he talked and ate as did the others, they changed
their minds and said that he was a god.

The news of a god spreads rapidly. The chief man of
the island, who had large estates near the shore and who
sheltered and lodged them for three days, had a father
ill with dysentery. Paul came into his room and prayed
and healed him. The Maltese were more convinced than
ever that gods had appeared and people came from all
over the island with their sick.

Paul and his companions spent the three months
of the Maltese winter disclaiming their godhead, preaching and healing. When the early spring came, they
boarded another ship from Alexandria which had been
wintering in the great harbor. They were heaped with
honors, and everything necessary was put on board for
their comfort.

The ship went north across the sea to Sicily, and remained at Syracuse three days. From there, by adept
tacking, they worked their way north through the
straits of Scylla and Charybdis and with the help of a
south wind came swiftly up the Italian coast.

Small ships from Puteoli which had been watching for
the first great ship of the Alexandrian fleet to come
through the spring mist, now sailed swiftly ahead to
announce their arrival and all the people of Puteoli
ran to the harbor to cheer the coming of Rome's bread.

Puteoli, in the shadow of Vesuvius, was a great harbor—to passengers it was the blessed earth again—but
grain ships carried their cargo on to Ostia, the port of
Rome. There it was transshipped to smaller vessels going
up the Tiber.

. . . Italy, the land of the Caesars and himself in
chains: it took all his faith to keep Paul from stumbling.
"My heart was very heavy. Where had the Lord led
me?"

There were Christians in Puteoli. Found by Luke or
Aristarchus, they consoled him with their joy. They
sent messengers, perhaps, to Rome, but Roman Christians had already been gathered by Epaphroditus who
had been sent by the Philippian church to wait on Paul.
Julius the centurion agreed to rest with his whole band
of soldiers and prisoners in Puteoli for seven days.

The humanity of Paul cancels time. In all the history
of men it is hard to find another with such a gift for
making friends. Out of storm and shipwreck and en-

forced companionship, Julius became his friend, and
the poor anonymous prisoners must have stood under
this blessing like a tree.

Nothing in Paul's letters is more touching than the
individuals whom he calls by name, all linked together
in trust and affection. They were that "sweet smell"
which always confirmed his faith in the present and
future. They loved him because he first loved them; his
letters were filled with this love. His friends filled the
highways of the empire. Everyone knew he was a demanding taskmaster, but such a man is strong enough
to build and be built upon. His friends shared his pris-
ons, and many others may have done as Aquila and
Priscilla did: "Put their necks in danger for my sake."

See him, enormously curious and alert, concerned,
vivid, swift in compassion, swift in anger, hating in-
justice, not surprised by anything the world did yet
never impassive; overwhelmed by the enormity of the
world's resistance to the compassion and joy of the
Christ, yet even in fatigue and despair finding his
strength again—everlastingly shaping his outer life to a
vision.

A prisoner of Rome. Yet first he was a prisoner of
Christ. Let the two be one and confirm the day when
all chains will be struck away.

When, in seven days, he went on with Julius, he was
a strange kind of prisoner coming to a strange kind of
prison surrounded on all sides by friends. When they
reached Capus, twenty miles from Puteoli, they found
men and women who had come from Rome to kiss

him. And at the Market of Appius, a two days' journey
from Rome, there were other Christians, poor men and
women who had left their work in Rome to meet him.
And at The Three Taverns, thirty miles from Rome,
others were waiting with affection and delight. "Be ye
kind to one another, tenderhearted, forgiving one
another, even as God for Christ's sake hath forgiven
you."

It was a small army which came on to Rome, almost
a triumphant procession, Julius and the soldiers and the
sacrificial prisoners caught up in these gleaming people
who had love as their food and faith as their guide.

The approach to Rome along the Appian Way was
white with villas and the towering tombs of old patri-
cian families. The great aqueduct of Claudius was more
impressive than a temple—and fourteen aqueducts
carrying 300 million gallons of water a day to the city
multiplied the impression. The seven hills of Rome were
crowned by the palaces of the emperors, the temples
of their gods, and the arenas which were metaphors of
man's cruelty to man and beast.

At the Porta Capena, they passed under the aqueduct which turned the stones of the road green with its
endless dripping. No vehicle on wheels was allowed
inside the gate, so men with carrying-chairs set up a
din for passengers, and market wagons fought for a
right to unload their produce.

Massive Rome on which his thoughts had dwelt so
long suddenly filled his horizon—and it was merely a

city after all, truculent, heavy, assertive, convinced
that the pragmatism of life demanded a hard imposition.
It was crowded, haphazard, filled with ancient hovels
and splendid villas. It was the city which Tacitus called
"that common sink into which everything infamous
and abominable flows like a torrent from all quarters
of the world."

It had none of the grace of Athens or the cities on
the Aegean. Only the muscular gods had temples in
Rome—though Cybele had by the sheer force of the
mystery of birth, growth, and death become the Magna
Mater, and ten years before Isis and Serapis had been
brought to Rome to give sanctuary to certain tenuous
movements of the spirit.

Julius delivered his prisoners to his superior officer in
the Peregrini whose headquarters were on the Caelian
Hill. Paul was received courteously and granted a citizen's right: *custodia libera.* He might choose his own
dwelling place and receive his friends. His only sign of
restraint was the soldier to whom he was chained day
and night.

The genius of Paul was his power to bring all chains,
all restrictions, all love, all tenderness, all good report
to his boundless sense of God's love.

It is hard to believe that his guards turned a deaf ear.

The average Roman lived in a tenement, six or seven
stories high, untrustworthy, uncomfortable, prone to
collapse in the night with a terrible roar. Water was

piped only to the lowest floor. The houses were redolent with abounding life. Paul's lodgings were thus knit into the heart of the city.

In spite of the warm greetings and the procession that had brought him into the city, Paul knew that the Christians in Rome had only the letter which he had written them by which to shape their opinion of him. Romans had come to Christianity along other paths than his. Factional disputes were as common as the human race. It was God's mercy that each man did not make his own footpath which no one else could follow.

For a time his spirits were heavy; shipwreck and danger and chains had been repeated too often. But he knew that if he called himself an "ambassador in chains," this gave him the right to speak boldly. He did not wish anyone to think that his sufferings were his own choice; they were to affirm some transcending truth.

In three days he asked the rulers of the Roman synagogues to come to him. Most Christians in Rome were Jews and all Jews in Rome had a measure of power. The agitated gestures of explusion made by Claudius had not really weakened their power, and their stern ethics, which included their refusal to worship the emperor or to attend the blood games in the arena, were tolerated and protected.

Paul spoke candidly to the synagogue rulers. He said he was in bonds because false charges had been made against him; that the priestly party—not his nation—had forced him to appeal to Caesar.

"For this reason I have asked to see you and speak

with you. It is because of the messianic hope that I am bound with these chains."

The synagogue rulers said they had heard nothing against him. He had not been attacked in letters from Jerusalem nor had Roman Jews heard anything amiss. They expressed a lively interest in hearing what he had to say. A day was arranged when a great number of them would come to hear him speak.

They came. He spoke and they questioned and argued from morning to evening. He reaped the old familiar harvest; some believed, some did not, some left in anger.

Here the *Book of Acts* comes to an end. "And Paul dwelt two whole years in his own lodgings, and received all who came to him, preaching the kingdom of God and teaching about the Lord Jesus quite openly, and unhindered."

Why did it end at this point? To give all the speculations would be to give mere speculation. Luke died. Luke intended to write another book on Paul's last years. Paul was acquitted and went on to Spain.

The letters he wrote from Rome were like glimpses into lighted windows. Epaphroditus had been sick "nigh unto death, but God had mercy on him and not on him only but on me also, lest I should have sorrow upon sorrow." To the Philippians he showed his heart as always. "I have learned, in whatsoever state I am, therewith to be content. I know both how to be abased, and I know how to abound: everywhere and in all things I am instructed both to be full and to be hungry, both to abound and to suffer need. I can do all things through Christ which strengtheneth me. . . . In everything by prayer and supplication, with thanksgiving, let your requests be made known unto God, and the peace of God which passeth all understanding shall keep your hearts and minds." All send greetings . . . his invariable expression for linking together.

To Timothy ("I have no one like him") he wrote, "Do thy diligence to come shortly unto me, for Demas has forsaken me, having loved this present world, and is departed unto Thessalonica. Only Luke is with me. Take Mark and bring him with thee. . . . The cloak that I left at Troas with Carpus, when thou comest bring with thee, and the books but especially the parchments. . . . Do thy diligence to come before winter."

His other churches, how did they fare? He thought of them daily, he embraced them all in his love: children sent into the world to make over the world.

Those he trusted went back and forth till they knew the look of all seas and all highways: Titus to Crete and Dalmatia, Tychicus to Ephesus, Epaphras to Colossae, Crescens to Galatia; strong and valiant men who had learned their lessons well.

Time may have worked against him. As the crisis in Judea deepened (James was stoned to death in 62 A.D., and the Christians abandoned Jerusalem for Pella across the Jordan so as not to be embroiled in the rising rebellion), the simple charges against him of riot may have taken on a darker color. He made Christianity the issue, and he whom riots followed as birds followed a sower of seed may indeed have died for his faith.

Clement of Rome, writing to the Corinthian church

around the year 96 A.D., said that "after that he had
been stoned, had preached in the east and in the west,
he won the noble renown which was the reward of his
faith, having taught righteousness unto the whole world
and having reached the farthest bounds of the west;
and when he had borne his testimony before the rulers,
so he departed from the world and went into the holy
place having been found a notable pattern of patient
endurance."

If he was exonerated in his first hearing but held on
new charges, he would be fettered like a criminal—"but
the word of God is not fettered." He knew that he was
"already being poured forth as an offering and the time
of departure was come."

Whenever and wherever he died, it was at the hand
of Nero.

By tradition Peter died at the same time.

Peter died by crucifixion in Nero's Circus having
been forced, it was said, to see his wife put to death first.

Paul stood with his guards on the Ostian Way outside
the gates of the city. As a citizen he was not put on the
cross. A headsman drew his sword and Paul knelt.

He was buried by a highway—he who had traveled
the roads of the empire.

He had already written his epitaph.

"Neither death nor life . . . nor things present nor
things to come, nor height nor depth nor any other
creature shall be able to separate us from the love of
God which is in Christ Jesus our Lord. Nay, in all these
things we are more than conquerors through him that
loved us."

ABOUT THE AUTHOR

Henrietta Buckmaster was born in Cleveland, Ohio, but has lived in New York City most of her life. She is the author of a number of distinguished novels, most of which have been translated into other languages. Among them are *And Walk in Love,* a novel about the Apostle Paul, and, most recently, *All the Living,* a novel on Shakespeare. Among her nonfiction books, *Let My People Go* is a classic study of the antislavery movement in this country.

She has received a number of awards for her books, including a Guggenheim Fellowship.